The Summer
Of '56

Roderick Heather

Published by New Generation Publishing in 2017

Copyright © Roderick Heather 2017

First Edition

The author asserts the moral right under the Copyright, Designs and Patents Act 1988 to be identified as the author of this work.

All Rights reserved. No part of this publication may be reproduced, stored in a retrieval system or transmitted, in any form or by any means without the prior consent of the author, nor be otherwise circulated in any form of binding or cover other than that which it is published and without a similar condition being imposed on the subsequent purchaser.

www.newgeneration-publishing.com

New Generation Publishing

Also by Roderick Heather:

The Iron Tsar
Russia from Red to Black
An Accidental Relationship

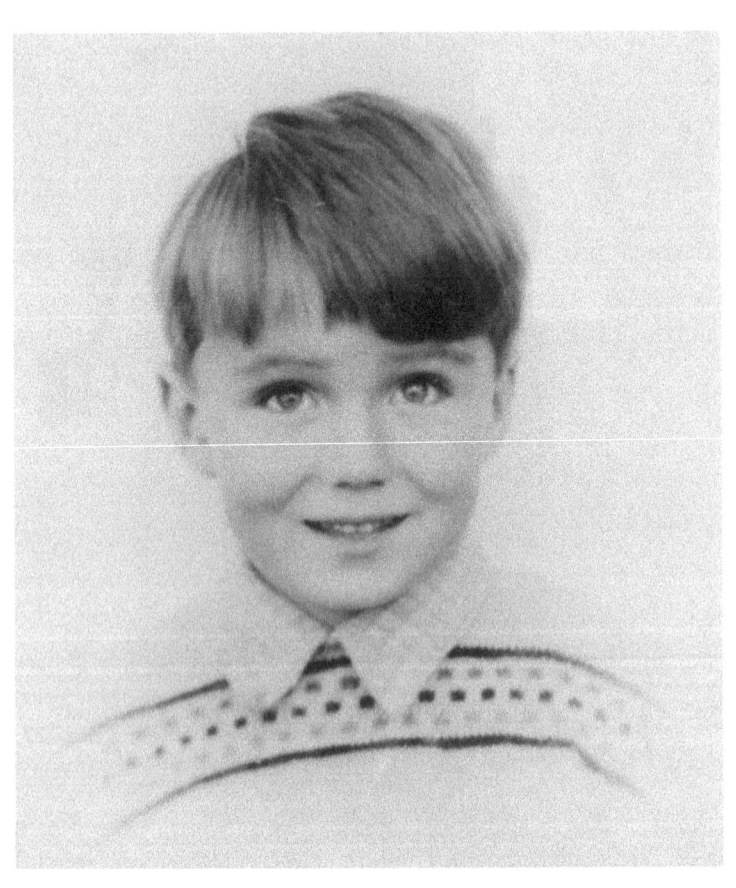

The Author

No-one is happy all the time and those who claim to be so are either fools or liars.

COVENTRY
Tile Hill
Earlsdon
Kirby Corner
Canley
Stivichall
Whitley
Willenhall
Westwood Heath
Burton Green
Baginton
King's Hill
COVENTRY
Kenilworth
Castle End
Stoneleigh
Bubbenhall
Stareton
Ashow
Leek Wootton
Hill Wootton
Blackdown
Weston under Wetherley
Cubbington
Lillington
Old Milverton
Milverton
ROYAL LEAMINGTON SPA
Offchurch
WARWICK
Radford Semele
Hampton on the Hill
Whitnash
A45
A4082
A452
A429
A46
A445
A425
B4101
B4113
B4115
B4453
B4455

Part One

1944 – 1956

The Early Years – A Tale of Two Cities

Chapter One
ATLANTIC CROSSINGS

When Norma Jean Mortenson legally changed her name on the 23rd of February 1956, it barely made the news. But when the renamed Marilyn Monroe married the playwright Arthur Miller just a few months later, it was a headline story in newspapers across the world. Not that it meant much to me at the time. I knew she was a glamorous American film star, an icon even, but the events of her life were only of passing interest to me. Monroe's recent films such as *The Seven Year Itch* and *Bus Stop* were not really the kind of thing an eleven-year-old boy watched. My periodic visits to the local cinema on Saturday mornings mostly revolved around Westerns or occasionally a Walt Disney cartoon. However, for my cousins, Brian and Pat, as well as my mother, the Monroe-Miller nuptials in June instantly became almost the only topic of conversation. In fact, 1956 had been an exciting year for those who followed the antics of film stars. Grace Kelly had married Prince Rainier of Monaco in April and the busty British film star, Diana Dors, had just sailed for New York to kick-start her Hollywood career. My mother used to read the *Daily Express* which is where I must have seen the reports of all these various events. In those days, the *Express* was a relatively conservative, broadsheet newspaper with reasonably good national and international news coverage – a distant cousin from today's publication. Although I rarely read much more than the front-page headlines, I always made sure I looked at my favourite part of the *Daily Express*, the fabulous Giles' cartoons [1] which I invariably found extremely amusing.

As the spring turned into the early months of summer in 1956, the media coverage of Marilyn Monroe's marriage was soon replaced by other headlines such as the abolition of the UK's death penalty and the first Eurovision song contest. The cricket season was in full swing and in the fourth Test Match of the Ashes at Old Trafford, Jim Laker set an extraordinary record by taking all of Australia's ten wickets - the first cricketer to do this in a single innings. My own achievements were much more mundane and for me, the year felt much like any other and life seemed to be continuing as normal. Sure, I had recently taken my Eleven-Plus exam and was now waiting for the results but my mother appeared more concerned about them than me. I knew they were important and would determine which senior school I moved onto later that September. However, I was confident in my childish naïveté that I would pass and go to a grammar school and I can't remember doing any extra work to prepare for the exam. My focus was much more on having fun and spending time with my school friends. I had also recently acquired a girlfriend which was a new experience for me and although she was no Marilyn Monroe and I certainly wasn't Arthur Miller, this relationship was something that I was keen to explore.

Although born in England in early September 1944, I spent my earliest years in the city of Toronto, Canada. My mother, Winifred, was a war bride, having married my father Bill Heather who was a Canadian bomber pilot serving in the Royal Air Force. My parents first met at a Saturday night dance in the early summer of 1943 at the Clarendon Hotel in the centre of Royal Leamington Spa. At the time, my mother was living there in a small rented flat in Lansdowne Crescent and my father had recently

---

[1] Ronald Giles cartoons which appeared in the *Daily Express* and *Sunday Express* were a national institution between the 1940s and 1980s.

been transferred from Yorkshire to the nearby RAF base of Gaydon [2]. After a relatively short courtship, they were married at the Leamington registry office. I don't know what sparked the initial attraction to each other but it was an unusual match in that my mother was thirty and almost five years older than my father. He was a lively, easy-going, good-looking young man from a well-to-do Toronto family and could no doubt have had his pick of any of the available young women in Leamington at the time. Although my mother was tall, slim and well-spoken, she was relatively quiet and reserved. She was cultured, enjoyed the theatre, opera and ballet and even spoke a little French. She was thus quite different in character and outlook from my father. My mother was also divorced, a quite uncommon thing at the time, at least among ordinary people. I don't know many details of her first marriage or why and when she divorced as she rarely ever spoke to me about it. The only facts I know are that the couple lived in the London area for a while before the War and that she and her first husband had a son who died soon after birth.

I was named after my father's younger brother Roderick John, who also served as a pilot officer but in an RCAF squadron flying out of Croft in North Yorkshire. He was sadly killed aged twenty-one during a night-time bombing raid over Germany in March 1943. That particular day, he was actually the navigator for a Wellington bomber of the 427th or Lion Squadron that was part of a major attack on Essen. Having reached the target, my uncle's plane was picked out by searchlights and then hit by shrapnel which instantly killed him and severely injured several other members of the crew as well as critically damaging the aircraft. Despite this, the crew managed to complete the raid and fly the crippled plane back to England. Rod had enlisted at the age of nineteen in August 1940 and was sent to Britain six months later, soon to be joined by my father. My uncle had an eventful and

---

[2] Gaydon is now the Heritage Motor Centre museum.

distinguished service record, having been mentioned in dispatches several times and surviving in a dinghy for many days at sea after he was shot down over the Channel. My father's letters to Rod at that time were all returned '*missing in* action'. As my mother later told me, my father was left totally distraught by the tragic loss of his younger brother. They had been very close and it took a long time for him to get over it. Rod's death occurred on the same day as my mother's birthday of March 12th and coincidentally, a generation later, it was also the date on which my first son was born. My uncle Rod was buried in a churchyard in Saffron Walden and many years later I went to visit his grave with my father – an extremely poignant moment for both of us. I also found it rather unnerving to be standing there, staring down at a tombstone with my own name on it, an eerie experience that I'm sure few people ever go through.

In the summer of 1945, my father was de-mobbed and left England to return to his home town of Toronto in Canada. My mother and I stayed on in her Lansdowne Crescent flat for a few months until we were able to follow my father across the Atlantic to a new world and a new life. She was just one of around 45,000 British women who went to Canada as war brides in the period from 1944 to 1947 and I was one of the 15,000 children who accompanied them. We sailed on a transport ship organized by the Canadian government and landed at Halifax, Nova Scotia from where we made the long train journey to Toronto. My father came from a relatively well-to-do Canadian family, my grandfather being a vice-president at General Motors, then the largest automotive company in the world. He and my grandmother lived in a fine home in a posh Toronto suburb just north of the city, together with my father's unmarried younger sister, Aunt Bonnie-Jean. My great-aunt, Jean, who lived in an apartment in the city centre, completed our immediate family group in Toronto. On his return to Canada, my father joined a government re-training programme for war veterans and soon had a job as an air traffic controller at the rapidly expanding Toronto international airport. We moved into a house in Merritt Avenue in Malton, a suburb to the west of the city, not far from the airport and there my mother settled down to adapt to her new life in Canada as a housewife and mother. The memories I have of my early childhood in Toronto are few and faded. I can recall our white, two-storey clapboard house in Merritt Avenue and the raised wooden boardwalks in some of the suburban streets, quite different from the solid pavements in England. The strongest memories are of the extremely heavy snowfalls in winter; great for a toddler like me to play in but challenging for my parents when we were snowed in. I can also vaguely remember the hot summer weekends and holidays when we used to drive up in my father's car to one of the myriad of small lakes north of the city. Due to my grandfather's connection with General Motors, we had a new car every year, usually a Buick or Chevrolet.

Although Toronto was a big city with a population then of around 650,000, it was as my mother later informed me, a far less sophisticated city than it is now and I don't think she found it easy to adapt to her new role of a suburban housewife. As an air traffic controller, my father regularly worked shifts so my mother was often alone in the evenings or at weekends. Things were also made more difficult by problems that developed in the family soon after our arrival in Canada. The fact that my mother was not only five years older than my father but also previously divorced seems to have been an issue in the family right from the start. In those days, divorce was not the common event it is now and a divorced woman in both British and Canadian society carried a certain stigma. As a result, my mother was never fully accepted by the rest of my father's family (apart from my Aunt Bonnie) and she felt increasingly isolated and unwanted.

Then my grandfather decided to run off with his twenty-one-year-old secretary and subsequently divorced my grandmother. When, perhaps predictably, my amorous grandfather died from a heart attack around a year later, he left the bulk of his estate to his erstwhile young bride. My grandmother received only a small settlement and of course, hopes of any inheritance by my father and my Aunt Bonnie disappeared overnight. Understandably, there was considerable bitterness within the family about my grandfather's behaviour, though I was totally unaware of this at the time. By pure chance, when visiting Toronto many years later in the late 1960's, I met the woman that my grandfather had abandoned us all for. Coincidentally, we were both attending a large drinks party given by an old family friend who introduced us to each other. It was hard to say which of us was the more surprised at this unexpected link back to past events but our initial awkwardness quickly faded and we chatted for a while. She was easy to talk to and seemed genuinely interested to hear about what had happened to my mother and me in the intervening years. Now in her late forties, she was still an attractive woman, quite tall with a slim figure, short light brown hair and a pleasant smile. Despite her evident charm, I felt it difficult to fully understand or forgive my grandfather's actions and the distress they caused within the family.

Some six months after my sister Fiona was born in July 1947, it became clear that she was not developing normally and she was eventually diagnosed with Down's syndrome, though in those days it was generally referred to as Mongolism. This unfortunate news brought increased tension at home, making life even more problematic for my mother. After lengthy discussions within the family, my father insisted that Fiona could only be properly looked after in a care-home but my distraught mother was totally against this. She refused to be separated from Fiona and eventually took the extremely difficult decision to leave my father and return to England with both Fiona and me. It was a pivotal moment in all our lives and certainly the wisdom of this move for everyone involved was something that I periodically reflected on as I grew older. Although my mother had a few friends in England, she had no savings, no close family to turn to for help and little idea of how she would make a living to support the three of us.

Despite the future difficulties that we would undoubtedly face, the irrevocable decision was made. So, in the early spring of 1949, together with my mother and young sister, I found myself on the Queen Mary, sailing back across the Atlantic from New York to Liverpool. We returned to Leamington (or Royal Leamington Spa if you wanted to sound posh) and initially found lodgings with an older couple in a small two-up, two-down Victorian brick terraced house in Cross Street, just round the corner from our previous flat in Lansdowne Crescent. My mother, sister and I shared the front bedroom and Nan and Pop as I came to call them had the other one at the back. Despite their unfortunate surname of Bastard, they were very kind to us and we effectively shared the whole house as one family. Pop kept racing pigeons in an extensive set of cages in the tiny back yard, just leaving enough room for the weekly Monday morning wash to be hung out to dry. His thinning hair was always combed straight back on his head, slick and shiny with Brylcream. We could usually tell when he had been out in the back yard with his pigeons as invariably there would be a couple of tiny grey feathers stuck to his greasy hair. Pop used to invite me to help him sometimes to feed his pigeons but I didn't really enjoy being surrounded by dozens of pecking, cooing and smelly birds. When at home, Pop invariably seemed to wander round in just a pair of trousers and a white vest with an old pair of patterned slippers on his feet. The only time I saw him in a shirt was on Saturday afternoons when he strolled across the road to the local pub, returning just in time for tea. Nan had greying hair, often in curlers and a slight stoop and she always wore the same well-used floral pinafore over her dress – I wondered if she actually went to bed wearing it. To my young eyes, she looked about eighty years old but was probably only in her fifties. She had evidently endured a hard life but was a kindly soul and looked after us all well.

Life with Nan and Pop in Cross Street introduced me to three new things – smoking, dentures and the weekly pools. My mother didn't smoke but both Nan and Pop did, like most adults in Britain at the time. In the evenings after tea, when we all usually squeezed into their small front room to listen to the radio, Nan and Pop sat there puffing away on their cigarettes until bedtime. Yet, I can't ever recall anyone objecting or leaving the room because of the smoky atmosphere. It was simply the way things were and it was almost universally accepted. Both Nan and Pop had dentures which was something I had never seen before. If I used the bathroom early in the morning, I would see their respective dentures sitting silently grinning at me from their separate glasses of water. I half expected them to start chattering away to each other. The last novelty I witnessed at Nan and Pop's was the tense excitement of the weekly pools ceremony on Saturday evenings, an experience shared with millions of other homes across Britain at that time. This was a system of betting on the results of the league football matches that day and was the only legal form of gambling then permitted in Britain. Organized by companies such as Littlewoods and Vernons, it was broadly similar to the National Lottery today, except that they didn't give any money to charitable causes. The winning weekly prize could be tens of thousands of pounds, a fortune in those days when the average annual wage was £100 and a decent house could be bought for £500. In addition, there were lots of smaller prizes every week ranging from hundreds of pounds down to a few shillings. Pop played religiously every week and each Saturday when he came home from the pub, he would disappear into the front room with his pools coupon and a fresh cup of tea to listen to the football results given out on the BBC's Light Programme. As far as I can recall, he never won anything but was always hopeful that next week would be different. It was this hope that kept Pop and millions of other people in Britain going from week to week; anyone could win and the dream of a life-changing win on the pools was a national obsession.

I was introduced to one other thing while living with Nan and Pop. Our front bedroom looked down into the street and almost directly opposite on the corner, was a large advertising hoarding which seemed to permanently feature a Guinness poster. Every night when I went to bed or each morning when I drew back the curtains, I couldn't help but see their advertisement. Despite this daily exposure over the several months of our stay in Cross Street, their persistent message '*Guinness is Good for You*' never persuaded me to try their beer, then or subsequently. However, the close proximity of the hoarding to the local pub opposite was presumably felt to be a good spot by the Guinness advertising people.

It was during our stay in Cross Street that my mother eventually decided that she could earn a living from dressmaking. I don't know what put this idea in her mind but the fact that we lived just round the corner from the Gor-Ray factory, then a well-known ladies fashion wear producer, may have been the inspirational spark. I am not sure either exactly how or from where my mother got her seamstress skills. When I later asked about it, she said she learnt to sew while mending her father's clothes. He was a salesman in the garment industry and although based in Birmingham where my mother was born, his wife had died quite early on in their marriage and as a young girl, my mother had subsequently accompanied him on his travels around the country. Whether true or not, this explanation could only have been part of the story; mending her father's clothes could not have given her the capability to design and make (often without a pattern) the range of women's clothing that she subsequently did. I know that at some stage during the War she worked on designing and making camouflage netting and so she presumably must have had some sewing skills by the time she started this war work. I also have a couple of old photos of me as a child in Canada dressed in a smart coat and shorts made by my mother so she clearly had good tailoring capability even then. Whatever the truth was, she was undoubtedly very talented and could produce all sorts of women's clothing as well as doing the more mundane alterations. Over time, she was able to build up quite an extensive client base across the Midlands and eventually made dresses for several well-known people.

Chapter Two
LIFE WITH OUR NEIGHBOURS

After several months in Cross Street, my mother eventually found a relatively spacious flat to rent on the first floor of a substantial white-stuccoed Victorian terraced house in Kenilworth Road, a couple of blocks north of Leamington's town centre. Our new flat, which was to be our home for the next six years, had the luxury of three bedrooms, a good-sized living room, a small, narrow kitchen plus a bathroom and a separate toilet. The large ground floor flat below us was occupied by an elderly Scottish lady, a Mrs Mitchell together with her spinster daughter, Isobel. The old lady was pleasant enough with my mother but her daughter always seemed aloof and quite unfriendly. She had bright carroty-red hair and a tightly drawn face with thin lips and a prominent, straight nose. Her demeanour and appearance probably explained why in her forties she was still single. We shared the same front door and wide entrance hall from which a set of broad stairs led up to our flat. Once through the front door, there was no separate entrance to our flat. At the top of the main staircase, a large, open landing gave access to either a few more steps leading up to our three front rooms or to the back passageway that led past the bathroom and our two rear bedrooms then on to the back stairs that went down to the rear door and yard.

The long, straight wooden bannister of the main staircase seemed purpose-made to me for sliding down but I soon learnt that this little pleasure could only be enjoyed when the Mitchells were not around. Peace and quiet were the order of the day in their domain and this wasn't to be ruined by the newly-arrived youngster upstairs. If I didn't close the door quietly on arriving home or made too much noise in the hallway, Isobel's angry, pinched face would mysteriously appear round her living room door. Words were rarely spoken but her stern glance was enough to send me scampering upstairs as fast as my young legs could carry me. In fact, I was a little scared of her and did my best to stay out of her way, no doubt to the benefit of both of us.

Our Leamington home was actually a *ménage à trois* as there was also a small attic flat on the second floor at the rear of the house. Presumably the servant's quarters originally, these rooms were rented out by my mother to supplement the money she was able to earn from her dress-making. Access to this flat was via a shared rear ground floor entrance and up two flights of uncarpeted, creaky wooden back stairs. The flat comprised a narrow, windowless small kitchen, a living room heated by a small gas fire plus a bedroom just large enough for a double bed and a wardrobe. There was no bathroom or toilet so the tenants had to come downstairs to share our bathroom on the first floor. Sharing the conveniences in this way was inconvenient for all of us. The attic flat was occupied by several families during our time at Kenilworth Road. The first tenants were a young Italian couple who, along with many of their countrymen, had immigrated to Britain in the late 1940s. They had come from the south of Italy and the man had been recruited to work in our local brick factory. They were a vivacious, friendly pair and with their dark black hair, olive skins and accented English, they seemed quite exotic to a youngster like me. The wife was a good cook and amongst other things, she taught my mother how to prepare genuine Italian-style spaghetti Bolognese, a recipe that I later learnt and still cook today. I can also remember them trying to teach me to count up to ten in Italian which remained my party trick for a while.

After a year or so, the Italians moved on and were replaced by an English couple, the Merricks. They were of a similar age to my mother and soon became good friends with her and were always kind to me. In fact, it was Mr

Merrick who patiently taught me how to ride my first bike in the small street behind our house. They were also the very first people I knew who had a television. It sat proudly on the sideboard in their living room and if there was something special on, we were invited upstairs to join them. We usually watched with the lights out as it was easier that way to see the black and white pictures on the screen. By today's standards, their nine inch TV seems ridiculously small and the picture quality was markedly inferior, yet it never spoiled our enjoyment of whatever was being broadcast by the BBC. As the flickering images danced around the darkened room, it somehow seemed to me as if the people on screen were actually there with us. *Come Dancing* and *What's My Line* were particular favourites of my mother's while I liked *Muffin the Mule*. Annette Mills (the sister of the actor John Mills) was the presenter and during a later visit to London, I was given a signed copy of her *Muffin the Mule* book. I also recall watching a horror film one evening. 'Watching' is perhaps not the right word as I spent a lot of the time behind the sofa, too scared to view it all. Otherwise, I was enthralled and enchanted by that magic box which brought the world to our living room – or at least, the Merrick's. Sadly, the Merricks and their TV eventually left for bigger and better accommodation across the other side of town.

Our final tenants were a TV-less Irish couple called the Husseys and their son, Dennis. He was a year or so older than me but shorter and wiry with a mop of dark, wavy hair. In those days, Dennis the Menace was a popular character in a boy's weekly magazine and I felt that my upstairs neighbour could easily have been the inspiration for the cartoon persona. With the arrival of the Husseys, Dennis and I became extremely close friends, spending much of our free time together, though as the family was Catholic, he went to a different school. Our principle playground was the alleyway that led from the back of our house plus the streets beyond. On wet days, we played our games inside on either the front or back stairs, often to the annoyance of the Mitchell ladies downstairs. There was a good-sized walled garden to the rear of the house but this belonged to the Mitchells. When we first moved into Kenilworth Road, we were allowed to use it and I have memories of enjoying picnics on the lawn on warm summer days with my mother and Fiona. However, for some reason that I never understood, we were banned from the garden after a couple of years by Mrs Mitchell and so subsequently, I had no qualms about making lots of noise when playing inside the house. With the garden beckoning from several of our windows, this was a difficult rule to constantly comply with for Brian and me. There was a large, old apple tree immediately outside Brian's bedroom window and occasionally, when we thought the Mitchells were out, we would climb out onto its branches and sneak down into the garden to play.

Mr Hussey worked as a builder's labourer in the town. He was a tall, gangling man with light brown hair who when sober was gentle and charming with a broad Irish smile and playful eyes. Sadly, when drunk, which he usually was on Saturday nights after payday (most people worked six days a week then), his mood changed totally and both Dennis and his wife especially suffered for it. Not long after they arrived, I bumped into Mr Hussey in the rear yard one Saturday night as he was coming home. He was a scary sight, swaying and staggering along and only the narrow confines of the alley walls kept him upright. He then urinated in the yard and when he saw me, he shouted out something but his words were too slurred for me to understand. I quickly scuttled off up the back stairs to the safety of our flat. After that, I tried to avoid going anywhere near the back stairs or yard on a Saturday night.

The shouting and screaming upstairs would normally start late in the evening when the inebriated Mr Hussey had finally managed to climb the stairs to the top flat. We were usually in bed when the upsetting sounds of loud and violent argument drifted down to our flat below. Most of the time, the noise would eventually subside after ten to fifteen minutes but occasionally, the shouts and screams by Mrs Hussey became more desperate and agitated. Sometimes my mother would put on her nightgown and go upstairs to try to mediate and calm things down; at other times, Mrs Hussey would escape downstairs to our flat. She would stand on the large landing outside our bedroom weeping and crying out for help, visibly shaking with fear until my mother went out to comfort her. On these occasions, they would go into the kitchen, my mother would make a pot of tea and there they would quietly sit until Mrs Hussey recovered and felt able to return upstairs. This respite usually allowed enough time to pass for her husband to fall asleep in a drunken stupor upstairs. However, I remember that on several occasions over the years, the situation became so serious that the police had to be called in to sort things out. The worst case was when Mr Hussey actually broke his wife's arm; he spent that particular night in the police cells.

In those days, domestic violence didn't receive the same attention from the police or the wider public as it might today. Unless there was exceptional or persistent violence, the police felt unable to interfere in what was seen simply as a domestic matter. The kind of support available today from charities, the local council's Social Services or counselling was all but non-existent then. Despite Mr Hussey's night in the cells, it wasn't long before another bout of Saturday night drinking led to the resumption of the shouting and screaming upstairs. These periodic events in the Hussey household were extremely upsetting for both my mother and me but their regularity must have been even worse for Dennis. As he slept on a pull-out bed in the living room of their flat, he must have often been in the thick of the arguments and violence. Yet he never commented or complained about it to me and in return, I never said anything to him. I suppose we both just accepted such happenings as part of our daily lives. At that age, there was nothing we could do anyway to change things.

Of course, most of the time things were quite normal. Mr Hussey was always cheery towards me if I went up to their flat looking for Dennis to come out to play. He would occasionally help us by doing the odd repair in our flat or try to sort out my bike when I had a problem with it. He used to grow tomatoes every year in the roof space above their kitchen. You had to stand on a stool and wriggle through a small hatch to gain access to the roof area but once inside, there was enough room overhead to move around. It also had a wide roof-light which provided just enough sunlight to allow the tomato plants to grow in their pots. It seemed a lot of effort to me for just a few semi-ripe tomatoes but as Mr Hussey once explained, it was a token replacement for the vegetable garden he enjoyed at their previous home in Ireland.

Mrs Hussey would occasionally come down to our flat to join my mother for a cup of afternoon tea and a chat. I think she was a very lonely person and I can't ever recall the Husseys having visitors while they lived upstairs. They had left their family and friends behind in Ireland when they emigrated to Britain and didn't seem to have made any friends in Leamington, even among the Irish community. Mrs Hussey was short in stature and her dark wavy hair already had strands of grey running through it. Like many women of her generation, she didn't work and being cooped up in her small flat all day must have been quite depressing. Coupled with the problems of her husband's heavy drinking, she led a difficult, rather isolated life. Her visits with my mother were a vital escape valve from the stress she was under. I well remember how these sessions would regularly end in her gently weeping while my mother patiently sympathized and tried to comfort her. Sometimes, in an effort to cheer herself up, Mrs Hussey would sing. She had a reasonable voice and her favourite was the ballad, *Danny Boy* which when she was in full flow, would echo mournfully round our flat. It made her think of Ireland which she clearly missed and I think she would have gone back, given half a chance. The

Welsh have a useful word for this deep longing for one's homeland, *hiraeth*. It has a much more evocative meaning than the English word homesickness, with a sense of yearning and nostalgia. I don't know if there is a similar word in Gaelic but it's definitely what the melancholic Mrs Hussey felt when she launched into this song.

The arrival of these Italian and Irish families as our tenants upstairs reflected what had been happening in the wider society of Britain both during and immediately after the War. The large influx of foreigners into Leamington actually started during the War. After the occupation of Czechoslovakia by Germany, many Czechs fled to Britain and some four thousand members of the Free Czechoslovak Army (FCA) were based in the Leamington area. Many of them trained as parachutists and carried out undercover missions behind enemy lines. Probably the most famous wartime action undertaken by the FCA was the assassination of the Nazi leader, Reinhard Heydrich, in a Prague suburb in May 1942. The four men who had carried out the shooting escaped and later found shelter in the crypt of a church in central Prague along with several other FCA men who had been parachuted into the region on previous covert missions. Unfortunately, their location was betrayed to the Nazis by a fellow Czech soldier and the church was soon besieged by seven hundred Waffen SS soldiers. The cornered Czech paratroopers held off the Germans for several hours until their ammunition was exhausted. Then, with their final bullets, they each chose to commit suicide by shooting themselves in the head rather than being captured by the SS. There is a moving memorial fountain commemorating the FCA and their war dead in the shape of a parachute in Leamington's Jephson Gardens.

Along with the Czechs, even greater numbers of Polish men and women escaped to Britain during the War, though there were relatively few of them based in wartime Leamington. My mother evidently knew some of these Polish and Czech soldiers as I can recall her talking about them with my grandmother in our Kenilworth Road flat. She spoke highly of their courage and bravery during the War. With the recovery of Britain's economy after the War, demand for labour rose beyond the country's own domestic supply potential and so the government began looking for ways to boost the labour pool. In the spring of 1946, the British wrote to every member of the Polish Armed Forces in the West, inviting them to settle in Britain and around 150,000 took up this offer. Over the ensuing couple of years, well over one hundred Polish men arrived in Leamington, initially living in camps and working on local farms. The Poles were subsequently joined by a number of Latvians and Ukrainians as well as by several former German prisoners of war who elected to stay on in Leamington. I well remember that one of the Germans even lived a few doors down the street from us in Kenilworth Road and ironically, he earned a living as a house painter[3]. Dennis and I called him Fritz but I don't think that was his real name.

The ongoing disruption and shortage of work in much of war-torn Europe encouraged workers from several other countries to migrate to Britain, especially from Italy and then increasingly, the Irish. However, all these new European arrivals were insufficient to meet the demand for labour and after The Royal Commission on Population report in 1949, the doors were opened to welcome workers from much wider sources, including the Caribbean and other Commonwealth countries. Although this rapid influx of people from the Commonwealth later led to rising racial tension in London and several other large cities, I don't recall Leamington experiencing much of these problems. The fact that there were plenty of jobs for everyone as well as initially an adequate housing stock (Leamington had not received much bomb damage during the War) no doubt helped in this respect.

---

[3] Ironic because Adolf Hitler was also a house painter.

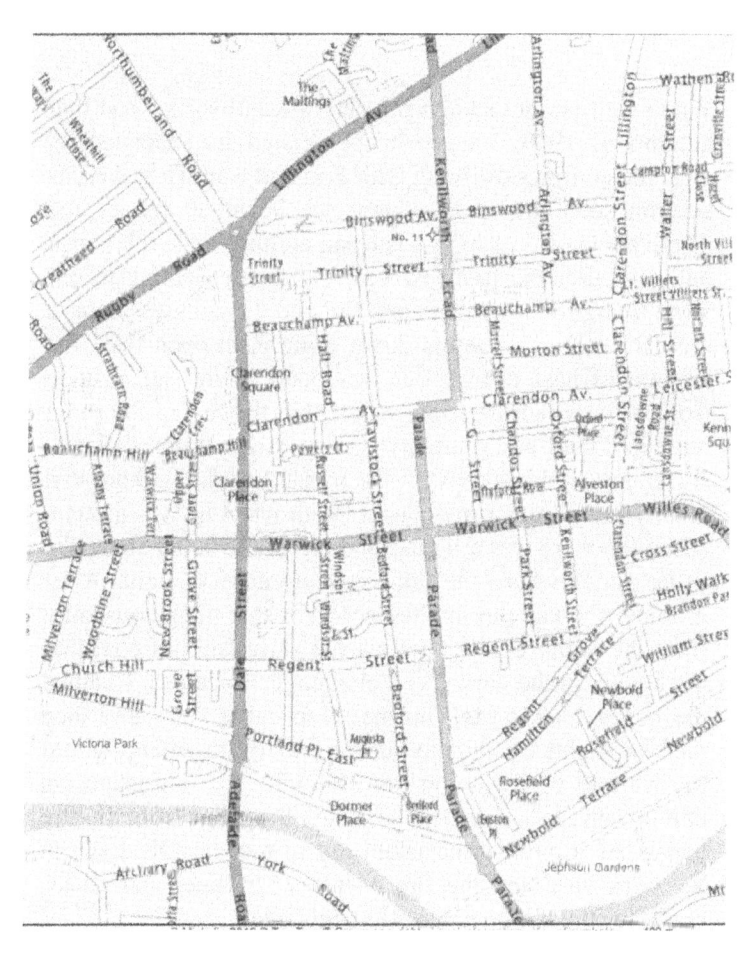

Leamington Spa Town Centre

Chapter Three
KENILWORTH ROAD

When we first moved into our flat in Kenilworth Road that autumn of 1949, we much appreciated its spaciousness after the confines of living with Pop and Nan. However, as autumn soon turned to winter, we began to realize the disadvantages of its high Victorian ceilings and wide, open hallways. For the first few years, the only heating in our large living room was an open fire and the coal was kept in the dark cellar two floors down. Like most open fires, the amount of heat thrown out was good if you sat right in front of it (which we usually did!) but the rest of the room remained cool and draughty. Going down to the cellar to fill up the coal bucket was an unwelcome daily chore that mostly fell to me or my cousin Brian when he was around. Although there was a light at the top of the cellar steps, the cellar room where the coal was stored was unlit. After groping my way through the cobwebs that hung constantly from the cellar ceiling, getting the shovelfuls of coal into the bucket in the dark was a challenge. Once full, I hauled the heavy bucket back up the steep cellar steps and then the two flights of stairs to our flat, finally re-emerging into the warmth of the living room looking like a Dickensian chimneysweep's boy. The next day, the ashes from the fire had to be removed and taken out to the dustbin down in the back yard and the fire re-laid with paper and sticks, ready for the whole process to begin again.

Although I hated this chore, we needed the heat and I always drew some compensatory pleasure from the daily ceremony of lighting the fire. There was something magical when the fire first crackled into life and the initial hint of warmth reached my outstretched hands. Like the touch of the sun on your face on a day in early spring, it provided a subtle feeling of well-being together with a regenerative sense of optimism. After three or four years of living in Kenilworth Road, my mother purchased a second-hand brown, square paraffin heater which was used in the living room to provide additional warmth during the winter months. Although its extra heat was welcome, it wasn't terribly efficient and had the distinct disadvantage of generating significant fumes as well as often being rather temperamental to light. It burned a special pink-coloured paraffin that was kept in a small jerry can in the hall. Periodically, a man from a local hardware shop would call round in his little old green Morris van to top up our supply.

In the kitchen, apart from the oven, there was no heating and the same went for the bathroom. Hot water came from either boiling the kettle in the kitchen or on Sunday bath nights, by firing up the unreliable and explosive gas geyser. Lighting this piece of early 20th century technology was invariably problematic; sometimes it worked and sometimes it didn't. And when it did, there was often a loud bang as it burst into fragile life and began heating the water - I was scared stiff by it. Heating the water for a bath was costly and so Brian and I usually shared as did my mother and Fiona. In winter, the body heat generated from the hot bath was quickly lost as we stood in the freezing cold bathroom to dry off and dress. At such times, I was glad that I only had to take a bath once a week. Without an entrance door to our part of the house the hallways and stairs were always draughty and cold. Although there were small gas fires installed in each of the hearths of the bedrooms, we were under strict instructions from my mother to only use them on the coldest of days and then solely for a few minutes while undressing. The only exception was on Christmas Day when my mother would turn on the fire in her bedroom for a couple of hours while we all opened up our presents. Our standby on really cold winter nights was a pair of identical ceramic, stoneware hot water bottles which were carefully allocated between us according to the time each of us went to bed. They were not particularly user-friendly in the way that the more modern rubberised hot water bottles are and one of them had a tendency to leak slightly if not kept upright. Since they were identical, you were never certain whether you had the leaker or not but overall, they did their job and made climbing into a cold bed slightly more bearable.

Our Kenilworth Road home was rented unfurnished so when we moved there, my mother had to beg, borrow and buy enough bits and pieces to make the place habitable. It was sparse but adequate initially and as time passed, additional items of furniture were acquired from local second-hand shops or 'on tick' [4] to gradually improve our level of comfort. Fortunately, with her sewing skills, she was able to make all the curtains and many of the soft furnishings herself. Most of the rooms had dark-stained, bare wooden floorboards except for the living room in which we had a large floral rug in the centre of the room and the bathroom which had a rather worn, brown linoleum covering on the floor. Although our flat was in generally good repair, it was not without problems. A couple of the old sash windows didn't close properly, leaving a gap at the top which in winter had to be filled with paper or old towels to stop the draughts. We had occasional problems with a persistent roof leak in the bathroom and a patch of penetrating damp on the wall of my mother's bedroom caused some of the plaster to fall off one day. I think my mother complained about each of these problems to the landlord but without result and we certainly didn't have the money to pay for repairs.

My mother did most of her dress-making in a corner of our living room, underneath a south-facing window overlooking the Mitchell's garden. She rarely had time to enjoy the view but the window's natural light was beneficial when she was doing a lot of fine stitching. Her

---

[4] A form of hire purchase, also known as never-never payments since the debt never seemed to be repaid.

work started early, sometimes six or seven in the morning if she was busy and would run through to the evening for five or six days a week. The usual household chores, cleaning, cooking, washing, shopping etc. were somehow fitted in to this routine. Sundays were mostly a day of rest with time for the family and to go to church. My mother usually listened to the BBC Light programme on the radio while she worked. At the time we had one of those iconic brown Bakelite table-top radios made by Bush with the woven gold effect speaker in the centre. She was a fan of Mrs Dale's Diary, I think partly because one of the characters ran a dress shop in Chelsea – something my mother would have loved to have done. She was also used to enjoy one of the comedy shows (I can't remember which one) and it was good to see her laughing occasionally.

Our living room also served as the cutting out and fitting room for my mother's work. If one of her clients was due to call, there was always a frantic clean-up. All the clippings of material and sewing cotton had to be swept up from the floor, other clients' work carefully folded and put on one side and any toys cleared away. My mother had a fascinating collection of all sorts and colours of buttons that she kept in a couple of large glass jars under her work table. She used these whenever a few new buttons were needed for a client's new dress or repair but when I was small, I found they were great to play with. I would empty out one of the jars onto the floor and sort them out into rows of similar colours, pretending they were my armies of soldiers on parade. There was a folding screen in one corner behind which clients could get changed when they came for a fitting or to try on the finished article. My mother would bustle around the client with a mouth full of pins, making small nip and tuck adjustments as required and marking the required hem length with a piece of tailor's chalk. Many of these fittings tool place in the evenings or at weekends when I was at home and initially I simply had to look away or watch the

TV as this process unfolded. However, when I got older, I was usually banished to the kitchen or sent out to play. In the summer, this was not a problem but in winter, having to leave the warmth of the living room fire to sit in the cold kitchen for half an hour was something I definitely disliked.

Apart from my mother, my sister and me, our Leamington flat also provided at different times a home to various relations, chiefly my older cousins Brian and Pat (actually my second cousins) and for a time, my great grandmother. Depending on who was in residence at any particular time, I either shared a double bed with Brian in his room or mostly a small single bed in my mother's room where she shared her double bed with my sister. My great grandmother, or 'Gran' as she was called, arrived a year or so after we had moved in to our Kenilworth Road flat and occupied the third bedroom at the end of the back hallway. For the past few years she had been living in Galley Common near Nuneaton with her youngest daughter and son-in-law, our Great Uncle Joe and Aunty Mary and it was they who arrived one Sunday afternoon to deliver Gran into our safekeeping. Gran reminded me very much of the enigmatic grandma character in Giles' cartoons in the *Daily Express*. Both shared the same overweight physique constrained in a plain black dress, flat greying hair that was tied back into a tight bun and rimless glasses as well as a biting tongue when things weren't going right. She suffered from pernicious anaemia and as a result her mobility became increasingly limited. Although she could walk around in the flat, she needed a wheelchair to go anywhere so never went out on her own. Taking her with us on our usual Sunday summer afternoon visits to the Royal Pump Room gardens or Victoria Park at the other end of town was a real challenge and not to be undertaken lightly. The mile or so outward journey was not too bad as it was mostly downhill but the return trip took the combined strength of my mother and me to slowly and wearily push Gran's wheelchair back up to

Kenilworth Road. Gran carried the remains of our picnic on her lap while all of us tried to keep an eye on my sister Fiona to make sure she didn't wander off. On arrival home from such an expedition, the traditional English cup of tea was rarely more welcome.

After a year or so living with us, Gran moved back to live with Uncle Joe and Aunt Mary in Galley Common. Joe and Mary arrived for tea one Sunday afternoon in their pre-war black Austin saloon and also brought with them my cousin Brian, who I had never met before. He was some five years older than me, rather short for his age, with dark straight hair and for the past couple of years he had been living with Joe and Mary, along with his sister Pat. They had been orphaned when they were quite young after both their parents were killed in a car accident. Brian and Pat had then lived in a children's home in the Birmingham area for a while until Joe and Mary who were childless had eventually taken them in. Early that evening when it was time for Joe and Mary to leave, it became evident to me that Gran was going back with them and Brian was now staying with us. No-one thought to tell me what had brought about this exchange of bodies but I later gathered that my mother had been finding it too much of a burden, both physically and financially looking after Gran. Although glad to be relieved of my wheelchair pushing duties, in a way I was sad to see her leave. I would miss her occasional little stories on a winter's evening as we sat in front of the coal fire, toasting bread on an old toasting fork which we then enjoyed covered with dripping from the weekend roast. When she left, Uncle Joe carried her battered brown leather suitcase out to his car and it seemed strange to think that this one small suitcase contained all her worldly possessions. However, this was not the last we would see of Gran as she returned some years later to live with us again when we moved to a new house on a council estate in Lillington, to the north of Leamington, in 1956. There, my wheelchair duties would once more resume.

A few months after Gran left and Brian arrived, we had another set of guests when my Great Aunt Laurie and her husband, Uncle Stan, from Auckland in New Zealand came to stay. Since they were due to live with us for six months, they took over Brian's room and he moved into the smaller back bedroom. I remained sleeping in my mother's bedroom. Although their stay was a long one, it proved not to be overly intrusive as they were off travelling a lot of the time, visiting other family and friends as well as many of the usual tourist sites in Britain. Until they arrived, I had no idea we had any relatives in New Zealand and although my mother probably explained it to me, I can't now recall exactly how we were related to Stan and Laurie. I later discovered that Laurie, who was actually my great aunt, had left Leamington around 1900 when she was just seventeen. She took a job as a nanny with an English family who were emigrating to New Zealand and made the long journey by steamship with them. Quite an adventure to undertake for a young seventeen-year-old. She later met her husband Stan in Auckland and this trip was her first visit 'back home'. Many years later, when I was on a business trip to Australia, I flew over to Auckland for the weekend to visit her. By then Stan had died and she was an old lady in her early nineties but she fondly remembered her visit to England and her extended stay with us.

During the whole of our time at Kenilworth Road, my sister, Fiona, remained permanently at home with my mother. If there were any local day care centres or organized activities for Down's syndrome children then, we were not aware of them. It was a very restricting life for both my mother and my sister. The extent to which children are affected by Down's syndrome varies enormously. With care and patience, the 'better ones' can be taught to read and write and have a reasonably independent life whilst those at the other end of the scale often suffer from additional health complications and need almost constant care and attention. Fiona was somewhere in the middle, fully capable of communicating and looking after her basic everyday needs but unable to read, although she would look through children's picture books and enjoyed colouring them in. She also had a good memory and knew her numbers as well as basic things such as which day of the week it was.

Fiona was small for her age, slight of build, with a freckled face and her father's light brown hair which my mother usually did into plaits. However, despite her size, she was physically quite strong. Fiona was a lively child with a mischievous sense of humour and surprisingly quick on her little legs when she wanted to be. Since she spent most of her days cooped up in our flat, I suppose it was only natural that she loved going out, whether for a walk to the park or to the shops. As soon as my mother started to put on her coat to go out, Fiona would jump up ready to accompany her. In this sense, she was like an excited dog that leaps up and starts wagging its tail as soon as the word 'walkies' is mentioned. Fiona's desire to escape from our flat into the world outside was a constant problem for us as she grew older. With no front door to our flat, it was easy for her to ostensibly go to the toilet or into the kitchen and then sneak off downstairs. If she made it that far without being discovered, once she was tall enough to reach the knob of the Yale lock on the entrance door to the house, she was out into the road in seconds. Usually, one of us would soon notice her absence and the urgent shout of 'Fiona's gone – she's out!' would echo around our flat. It was the cry we all dreaded, the equivalent of '*all hands on deck*' in our household. We would immediately stop whatever we were doing, rush downstairs and start running along the street in search of Fiona. If my mother was doing a fitting with one of her clients, she just had to abandon them in our living room with a hasty apology.

We would race down Kenilworth Road and head towards her usual destination, the town centre shops. Most of the time one of us caught up with her fairly quickly and she would be laughing and giggling as she always thought this was a great game. If she wasn't anywhere to be seen after ten or fifteen minutes of frantically running around the streets, we would return home to collect our bikes and the search would then be widened with my mother and I setting off in opposite directions. On these occasions, my mother's desperate anxiety was plain to see. All mothers worry when their child disappears but Fiona was especially vulnerable, she had no fear of strangers and would talk to anyone who stopped to speak to her. Also, she had absolutely no traffic sense and her favourite haunts of Kenilworth Road and The Parade were some of the busiest streets in Leamington. Despite our best endeavours, there were a couple of times when Fiona could not be found and my mother had to then call in the police who eventually tracked her down. The first time she was outside a toy shop in Regent Street where a small group of people were anxiously trying to find out who she was. Much more worrying was the second time when the police found her several hours later over a mile away near Victoria Park. She was walking along the street with a man who told the police he was trying to find out where she lived and take her home. Whether this was true or not was impossible to verify and the police simply brought her home. After this episode, we were extra vigilant with Fiona but short of tying her up, there was no way of preventing her occasional forays into the world outside.

At the back of our house, there was a long alleyway that ran behind the houses of our immediate neighbours and came out into a quiet side street. The alleyway and the adjacent street area were essentially my back yard and this was where I spent a lot of my free time. One summer's afternoon, when I was perhaps seven or eight, I was out there playing. I had found a six-inch square piece of roof slate that for several minutes I had been trying unsuccessfully to break in half by hitting it with a stone. Sitting on the edge of the pavement, I was so deeply engrossed in my childish pursuit that I hardly noticed a youngish man walking slowly along the pavement towards me. Only when he crouched down right in front of me did he come fully into my field of view. He asked me what I was doing and when I quickly explained my problem, he told me I needed some liquid to soften the slate – it would then crack more easily he said. I hadn't considered this intelligent application of science but as I didn't have any water, this was not an immediate solution. The kind man then said he might have the answer.

I'd never seen a man's penis before, certainly not one that was fully erect, so I was both curious and impressed when he unbuttoned his fly and pulled his out. I was even more in awe when after rubbing his penis for a short while over my slate, liquid began to emerge from it. A few seconds later, once the liquid had stopped flowing, he stood up and put his penis back into his trousers. My new friend then picked up my stone and smashed it into the slate, breaking it into several pieces right in front of my eyes. Not quite what I had wanted but impressive nonetheless. 'A little magic trick' he told me as he stood back to admire his handiwork, something to keep secret between the two of us. And with that remark, he turned around and sauntered off down the street. I wasn't sure what to say or do and so remained sitting on the ground for a while gazing at my broken slate in the gutter. Since my original task had now been more or less accomplished, I decided to head back to my house and see if there was anything for tea.

Once inside, I found my mother in the kitchen making some sandwiches for my sister and me so I sat down on a stool to wait. As she buttered the bread, she asked me what I had been doing all afternoon and I explained that I had simply been playing in the back alley. As I sat there hungrily anticipating my sandwich, I then added that a man in the street had just shown me a new trick and I elucidated on how he had broken the slate. This statement just popped out innocently. I wasn't supposed to share the secret but I suppose I was trying to impress on my mother that I had learnt something that afternoon while messing about in the street. The reaction I got was not what I had expected; my mother cried out and the knife slipped out of her hand onto the table. I was disappointed as that knife was about to enter the jam pot and spread delicious home-made raspberry jam all over my sandwich. Is the man still out there, my mother asked? I wasn't sure but she grabbed my hand and rushed the pair of us out of the house, down the alley and out into the street. Naturally, my erstwhile friend was nowhere to be seen. Once back in the kitchen, I received the statutory warning from my mother about staying away from strange men and if I saw him again, I was to immediately come and tell her. I failed to understand what the problem was and therefore couldn't grasp why my mother was so upset but her serious tone left me in no doubt that something awful had occurred that mustn't happen again.

Of course, what this unknown young man did was plainly wrong, taking advantage of my childish innocence. I have no way of knowing whether this was a one-off event or if he was a serial sex offender or potential child-molester who needed treatment or jail. However, was this a life-changing experience for me? Was it something that affected me for the rest of my life? The answer to both questions is no, at least as far as I am aware. The man never actually touched or threatened me and in fact, I had more or less forgotten the whole episode within a couple of days and my mother certainly never mentioned the subject again. In today's world, the police would probably be called out to investigate, with the whole incident possibly being reported in the local paper and I would be sent off for counselling. All of which would have had the effect on me of making the event a lot more serious than it actually was.

Chapter Four
THE VISIT

My early education years were spent at the local Milverton School on Rugby Road, about a ten-minute walk from our house and both my cousins, Brian and Pat, also went there while they were living with us. It was a typical late 19th century brick-built school with separate buildings for infants, juniors and seniors that drew from a very mixed catchment. The street with many of the wealthiest homes in Leamington was just around the corner whilst almost directly opposite was a row of what were essentially Victorian tenement buildings. I enjoyed my time at Milverton, mastering the basics of reading, writing and arithmetic as well as making some good friends in my class. There was a large central playground which we all used to run around at morning break and lunchtimes but no sports field. Once a week, each junior and senior class would walk the mile or so down to Victoria Park for their afternoon of games and sports. Little did I know then that I would return to my old school some ten years later, not as a pupil but as a student teacher in the junior section. The school had remained much the same in the intervening years and it felt very strange to find myself standing at the front of the classrooms in which I had first sat learning my three 'R's'. If the old buildings hadn't changed, fortunately the teachers had, so there was no-one from my pupil days to remind me what an unruly boy I was. Although I later decided that the teaching profession was not for me, I spent six of the happiest months of my life there.

When I started at Milverton, I quickly got to know a boy in my class called Michael who lived around the corner from me and we soon became best friends. His father had a grey, two-litre Standard Vanguard with red leather seats, quite a fancy car in those days and often at weekends I would go around and help Michael and his Dad to clean and polish it. Occasionally, I would be invited to join the family for a drive out somewhere for a picnic or a walk by the river in Stratford. It was the only time I ever got to travel in a car in those days and I loved being driven around in it. When not riding around in the Standard Vanguard, Michael and I made do with his little red pedal-car. Not as fast but great fun in their back garden nonetheless.

Late one winter's afternoon as I was walking home from Michael's, I saw another boy I knew running towards me down the street. As he went by, he shouted out excitedly that there was a house on fire around the corner and he was racing home to tell his brother to come and watch. 'Great', I thought to myself, 'I don't want to miss this' and as young boys do when pretending to be riding a horse, I slapped my thigh and speeded up down the street. I rounded the corner and looked down Kenilworth Road and sure enough there was a bright red fire engine with its lights flashing and hoses laid out across the pavement. Several firemen were running in and out of a house with smoke coming from an upstairs window. It took a couple of seconds to hit me but I suddenly realized that it was our house that was on fire and as I drew nearer, I could see my mother and Fiona standing outside the front door alongside Mrs Mitchell. In that instant, my mind swung from a feeling of terrific excitement through to one of fear and terror.

With my heart pounding, I rushed along the road and into the front garden to join my mother and sister. 'What's happening' I managed to blurt out rather breathlessly. My mother explained that the living room chimney had caught fire about half an hour earlier. She had lit the fire for the evening when suddenly a big puff of dense smoke came down out of the chimney followed a few seconds later by a ball of fire that flew out into the hearth. A subsequent roaring coming from inside the chimney was a clear indication that it was on fire and so my mother had called the Fire Brigade who arrived quickly and soon had things under control. It turned out that my mother hadn't organized for the chimney to be swept that year and so excess soot in the chimney had caught fire. After a while the firemen declared all was safe inside and we could go back in. The whole flat reeked of smoke and the living room floor nearest the fireplace was awash with water and it took several days before things were fully dried out and the acrid smell disappeared. After that, my mother was more assiduous about remembering to have the chimney swept annually.

Sadly, my friendship with Michael came to an end when his father took a new job in Hong Kong a couple of years later. At the age of seven, Hong Kong seemed a world away which I suppose it was. At the family's leaving party, Michael and I promised we would stay in touch and write to each other but predictably, the correspondence didn't last longer than a few letters as new horizons opened up for each of us. Michael and his family did however return briefly on home leave a couple of years later. They organized a reunion party in a private room of a café on The Parade and after copious sandwiches and cakes, Michael's father put on a slide show using a lantern projector with glass slides. For me and probably most of the other children who were present, this was the first time we had seen a magic lantern show and we all marvelled at the fascinating pictures of a distant and very exotic Hong Kong. The following day, Michael and his family returned to their different world and sadly, that was the last I ever saw of them. However, those exciting images of Hong Kong somehow remained at the back of my mind so that when I reached the end of my school days and had to think about a future career, I almost decided to take a job out there. Instead, it was the teaching position at Milverton School that finally won out, although eventually neither proved to be my final career choice.

After three happy years at Milverton, my mother received a letter one summer's day from the Warwickshire Education Department informing her that in September I was to move to a new junior school that had opened the year before in Lillington. Originally a separate village some two miles north of Leamington, Lillington was now effectively a suburb as row after row of newly-built private and council houses gradually filled in the intervening, previously green spaces. We were not consulted about this change in my schooling and we never knew how this unwelcome decision was arrived at within the Education Department. Not only was I forced to leave many of my school friends behind but as we quickly found out, actually getting to my new place of learning would prove to be a problem. My mother was told there was a bus that went to Lillington from a stop further along Kenilworth Road from our flat and so this initially seemed to be an adequate solution for my journey.

Unfortunately, the bus service in the mornings proved to rather erratic and in the first two weeks I was late for class several times – not the best start at my new school. It was obvious that an alternative transport method was needed. Although I had a small child's bike, it had no gears and certainly wasn't up to doing the journey on a daily basis. So the next Saturday morning, my mother took me to a bike shop in town where I was equipped with a replacement second-hand Raleigh bike that was not only bigger but had three Sturmey-Archer gears. I was in heaven and with my new independence, the world now seemed to be my oyster. However, there were two drawbacks. Firstly, my new bike had to be bought 'on tick' with payments spread over two years which was an unforeseen financial burden that my mother could have done without. Secondly, it meant that I now had to come home each day for my lunch instead of having it at school as I had been doing previously, both at Milverton and now Lillington. By doing this, we would cut out the cost of the school lunches as well as my bus fares and these savings would go towards the weekly bike payments.

One afternoon when I was eight, I arrived home from school, there was a man sitting on our couch in the living room chatting away to my mother. At first, I was very surprised as she never had a male visitor before but my surprise turned to puzzlement as his face somehow seemed familiar to me. My mother glanced up to see me standing at the doorway and beckoning me over said calmly and simply 'Your father is here, he's come to visit us'. Then things clicked in my young brain and memories of my father in Canada several years before pushed into my head. I never knew why my mother hadn't mentioned to me earlier that my father would be arriving that day. She wasn't a secretive person and as she told me later, she knew he was coming because he had written to tell her of his plans. I knew that they sometimes wrote to each other because I saw the occasional air mail letter from Canada in my mother's bedroom. They were the pre-printed ones using wafer-thin, blue paper that were the norm for airmail letters in those days. Maybe she had been uncertain of the exact day he would arrive, given the vagaries of transatlantic travel in those days, or just possibly whether he would come at all. Whatever the reason, I was taken completely by surprise and a variety of emotions and questions started swirling around in my mind. Of course, I was pleased to see my father again but I wasn't sure what to say or do. Why was he here, what did his visit mean, where would he be staying and for how long? In due time, all my questions were answered.

As my father sat there talking to my mother, he occasionally put his hand into his coat pocket and pulled something out that he then popped into his mouth and ate. Curious as to what he might be eating, I watched intently each time his hand went into his pocket and after a while my father realized what I was doing. He then pulled a small white paper bag from his pocket and held it out, nodding for me to try the contents. It was a bag of salted cashew nuts that he had bought in Woolworths on his way to our house. I had never tasted cashew nuts before and tentatively reached into the bag to try one. It was delicious and I eagerly reached into the proffered bag again and took out a few more. My father took hold of my hand and pressed it around the paper bag, saying in his soft Canadian drawl that since I evidently liked them, I could keep the rest for later. That moment of brief physical contact with my father and his gift of the nuts somehow raised a questioning hope inside me that perhaps he had come to stay permanently. A short while later, my parents' conversation seemed at an end and my father got up to leave. I went downstairs with him to the front door to see him off and as he left, he said to my delight, 'See you tomorrow'.

As I then found out from my mother upstairs, he was in Leamington for a couple of days, staying in a hotel on The Parade and would be back tomorrow morning to spend the day with us. What she didn't tell me then but I learned much later on, was that my father had mainly come to see if there was any chance of them getting back together again. After breakfast the next morning, I glued myself to the kitchen window to wait for my father's return. Eventually, a grey Ford Prefect four-door saloon pulled up outside the house and out popped my father; he had hired a car for two days so that he could take the four of us out. On the first day, we visited Warwick and its famous castle, then we drove on to Stratford for the Shakespearian sights plus lunch in a café and finally meandered back home through some of the local small villages.

The rented car wasn't exactly new and had clearly been around the block a few times but I felt happy to be enjoying the rare experience of being out in a car again and even more so to be doing it as a family with my father. He wasn't totally comfortable with the car – he was used to driving an automatic - and crunched the gears a few times as we rolled along but he became really annoyed with the windscreen wipers. When we headed back from

Stratford it started to rain and as we were climbing a long steep rise, the windscreen wipers moved more and more slowly across the windscreen until near the top of the hill, they virtually stopped. My father, unable to see out of the windscreen came as near to swearing as I ever heard him, while running through a gamut of criticism of the British car industry, British roads and the British weather. Finally, as we crested the rise and started going downhill, the wipers started to work again and gave no more problems for the rest of the journey. As my father found out the next day when he returned the car and complained, this was a design problem on all Ford Prefects of that period.

The next day, my father came again in the afternoon and we drove out to Evesham where my father wanted to visit a used car dealer that specialized in old British sports cars – he was interested in buying an Austin Healey or Jaguar XK120 to ship back to Canada. We chatted on the journey, he asked about my school and how I was getting on there and gave me few fatherly words of advice about working hard if I wanted to get a good job. I'm not sure that they had any particular effect on me but the fact that I remember them shows that his words must have gone into my brain somewhere. That evening, my parents went out together for dinner to a restaurant in the town centre. It was one of the very rare occasions that Fiona and I were left alone in our Kenilworth Road flat. Before going out, my mother asked me if it was OK and said it was important for her to have some time alone with my father. I didn't mind, I had just discovered a large cardboard box earlier that evening which I was busy converting into a make-believe army tank so was quite happy to be left to play and look after Fiona. When they came back after a couple of hours, they both seemed in good spirits and while Fiona and I then went to bed, they remained talking in our living room.

I took all this as a positive sign. Our couple of days together seemed to have gone well, my parents appeared to be at ease with each other and I was happy to see my father again. However, when my father reappeared later the next morning, it soon became clear that he was returning to Canada. My parents went into the kitchen where they talked for a few minutes and then my father came out, gave me a hug and saying it was now time for him to leave, wished me goodbye. While my mother went downstairs to the front door to see him off, I rushed to the living room window to catch a last glimpse of my father as he walked away down the street to catch the train to London. I was shocked and extremely disappointed and initially couldn't believe that he had really gone. When my mother came back upstairs, evidently a little upset, I asked what had happened. She replied that it was complicated; although she and my father still had affection for each other, Fiona was still an issue and getting back together at the moment just wasn't feasible. Sad as I was at this outcome, those last few words gave me a slight hope that maybe they would change their minds in the future.

Perhaps I should have guessed that something was up before my father arrived, as a couple of weeks earlier, my mother had bought me a new suit, my first and only one until I was at university many years later. She had ordered it like many other things in our house 'on tick' from the little man in glasses who used to call every month with his big black book. The suit jacket and short trousers were made of wool in a light brown and yellow check pattern. My mother was pleased with my new, smart appearance but I didn't like it much (it really wasn't me) and the woven wool cloth made my wrists and legs itch. Under my mother's guidance, I had worn it to church the following Sunday and then again when we went out in the car for the day with my father. After he had left to return to Canada, I was happy to see my suit carefully hung away in my mother's wardrobe. A few weeks later, my mother unfortunately fell ill again with one of her heavy bouts of flu and was confined to bed for almost a week. We had no money and little food in the house and one afternoon when I arrived back from school and went into her bedroom, I was surprised to see my jacket and shorts laid out on her bed. I thought at first she was going to make me wear it again the next day for school but she called me over and pushed the suit into my hands and told me to take it to sell at Joan's pawn shop in town. She gave me strict instructions as to how much I was to try to get for it, together with a list of a few items of food I was to buy with some of the money. Inwardly I was pleased at the thought of getting rid of these clothes but I could tell this was a difficult decision for my mother and her evident sadness made me unhappy too. We both knew that we wouldn't get anything like the original cost of the suit and to add insult to injury, she would have to continue to pay the remaining monthly instalments for some time yet. I went down to Joan's, successfully pawned the suit, bought the food and trundled home crying, not for the loss of my new suit but for my mother, the difficulties of our life and the fact that my father had gone back to Canada.

Chapter Five
HOLIDAY EXPERIENCES

Like many other people in Britain at this time, the horizons of our day-to-day world were very limited and almost our whole lives were mostly spent within a small radius of our home. Britain's expanding overseas trade provided occasional opportunities for families like Michael's to travel abroad, as did the nation's diminishing but still significant colonial and military responsibilities. But the days of cheap package holidays and mass travel were a long way off in the future; few people had the time or money even if they had the aspiration. For me, it was a ten-minute walk to school, the same to the shops of The Parade, Leamington's main street or the church on Sundays and most of my friends were no more than a ten-minute bike ride away. We only once went away on holiday as a family when my mother, sister and I travelled to the south coast by train one summer to stay with an old friend of my mother's for a week. I was six or seven at the time and don't remember much apart from the interminably long train journey and the excitement of climbing a large apple tree that grew in our host's garden. Otherwise, our annual family 'holiday' was a day trip during my school summer break on one of the many coach tours that operated out of Leamington at that time. We travelled to such exotic destinations as New Brighton near Birkenhead, Aberystwyth on the mid-Wales coast, the Malvern Hills in Worcestershire or Whipsnade Zoo near Luton. One of the good things about these trips was that we could wait to see what the weather was going to be like before booking so my memories are generally of sunny days at the beach or wherever. Although the journeys were tediously long, usually three to four hours in each direction, I enjoyed these one-day excursions. There was invariably an air of anticipation on the coach for the outward journey and there were always other children on the bus to play with once we reached our destination. On the return, a relaxed, convivial atmosphere with most of the passengers joining in the singing of songs such as *Ten Green Bottles* and *This Man Went to Mow* helped pass the time.

While we were at Kenilworth Road I also went down to London a couple of times to stay with some old friends of my mother's, the Bishops or Auntie Doreen and Uncle Bernard as I called them. They had met my mother during the War when Bernard and my mother worked together on designing and making camouflage netting. Bernard was an arts teacher which is presumably why he was allocated this particular war-time role. They became close friends with my parents and had stayed in touch with my mother while she was in Canada and after her return to England. They were now both teachers and lived in a small rented flat in Notting Hill which at that time was a far cry from the very affluent London suburb of today. It had received significant bomb damage during the War – there was a bombed-out lot almost opposite Doreen and Bernard's flat – and little rebuilding work had yet been undertaken. By the 1950s, many of the once-grand large Victorian homes in Notting Hill had been converted to provide cheap, multi-occupancy flats for rent. Inevitably, the low rents attracted an increasing number of immigrants to the area, especially those from the West Indies. The notoriety of Notting Hill was epitomised by the 1953 trial and execution of the notorious serial killer, John Cristie, who murdered at least eight women at his home in Rillington Place and the activities of the infamous racketeering landlord, Peter Rachman.[5]

On my first visit to Notting Hill during the summer holidays of 1952, I went down by train together with my

---

[5] At his peak Rachman had over 100 properties in the west London area as well as several night clubs.

cousin Brian. My mother walked us to the station in Leamington and as she settled us down in our seats on the train, she asked us to behave and reminded us of where we had to change en route and our instructions as to what to do on our arrival at Paddington Station. If Doreen and Bernard were not on the platform when we got off the train, we were to wait for them underneath the large station clock. It seemed straightforward enough to Brian and I, at least until we arrived at Paddington in the early evening rush-hour. My aunt and uncle were not on the platform waiting for us so we wandered off through the ticket barrier to look for the station clock. Somehow, the noise and bustle of the station plus the excitement of actually being in London must have affected our minds and vision. Although it's an extremely large, double-sided clock mounted high on the station wall, we missed it and sauntered off carrying our small suitcases in the opposite direction. It simply didn't occur to either of us to ask someone where the station clock was, we simply continued unperturbed walking up and down expecting to see Doreen and Bernard at any moment.

After wandering around aimlessly in the crowds for about quarter of an hour, we finally saw the clock but neither my aunt nor my uncle was there. Unsure now what to do, we noticed a sign to the station waiting room and decided that would be the best place to go. So, we went in and sat down, waiting to be collected. Some ten minutes passed before a frantic-looking Doreen, accompanied by a rather out-of-breath station master, burst into the waiting room and ran anxiously towards us. Brian and I were then subjected to a barrage of questions – where had we been, why didn't we come to the clock, were we alright? Doreen explained that she and Bernard had driven to the station to meet us but had problems finding somewhere to park so my uncle had waited in the car outside while my aunt came in to wait under the appointed clock. When we hadn't shown up, she had gone off to a telephone box and called my mother to make sure that we were indeed on the train. Worried that something serious might have happened to us, she had then sought help from the station master and the pair of them had been racing around the station trying to find us. Brian and I couldn't understand what all the fuss was about. In our naïveté, we didn't realize the potential dangers for two unaccompanied children wandering around Paddington station; we were simply glad to have now been found.

It wasn't the best of starts for our few days' stay in London but fortunately things then went fairly smoothly. Doreen and Bernard were childless, so looking after two young boys was a novel experience for them. Doreen was tall and blonde, very talkative and always full of questions about our life in Leamington. Bernard was slightly shorter than his wife, especially when she wore high heels. He was also much quieter and extraordinarily patient. At home, his nose was almost always in a book, at least until disturbed by a question or instruction from Doreen who definitely ruled the roost. Over the next three days, my aunt and uncle kindly drove Brian and me around in their car to see many of the famous central London sights as well as visiting a couple of the museums on the tube. I was both excited and fascinated by my first visit to London – the sheer size of the city, the huge number of people everywhere, the traffic and underground system and so many shops. The only disappointment was the fact that we were not allowed out of the flat on our own. At home, we were both used to wandering around the streets at will and I particularly wanted to explore the nearby bomb sight. But with Doreen strongly insisting that it was not safe for us to go out by ourselves, I was limited to exploring the Notting Hill street scene from the living room window. However, the fact that we were able to watch my aunt and uncle's television each evening was a partial compensation for our enforced confinement.

My second trip to stay with Doreen and Bernard was for New Year some eighteen months later. They had driven up to Leamington to visit us for Christmas 1953 and took me back down in their car for a few days. Bernard had recently acquired a new dark grey Ford Anglia which provided the excuse to come to see us. Recently introduced by Ford, it had a modern three box design but only a three-speed gearbox with a top speed that barely reached 70mph and it took a full thirty seconds to hit 60mph. It was probably fine around London but for the long cross-country journey up to Leamington, its performance was limited. In addition, a radio and heater were optional equipment and Bernard's car had neither. An hour or so after we had set out southwards along the A5 in the late afternoon, we hit fog which became more and more dense the further we went. Our progress dropped to a crawl which probably suited the Anglia but with only limited forward motion, meant that no engine heat penetrated the car. While Bernard doggedly kept the car moving forward, peering silently into the murkiness while my Aunt retreated into her overcoat and hardly said a word. It was the only time that I can remember the normally voluble Doreen not having anything to say. Huddled up on the back seat, I got colder and colder. With no radio to entertain us, our silent, misty journey became increasingly oppressive as the hours dragged by. Eventually, we emerged from the dark into the hazy streetlights of the London suburbs, reaching Notting Hill over six hours after we had set out from Leamington. We were all frozen and very tired and after a cup of tea, went straight to bed. Even with a hot water bottle in bed that night, it took a long time for my body temperature to return to its normal level.

I have only one other clear memory from this second stay in London with Doreen and Bernard which revolved around Muffin the Mule who was a character from a well-known children's TV programme in the 1950s. My aunt and uncle had remembered that I enjoyed watching it during my previous visit and had bought me a Muffin the Mule story-book as a late Christmas present. Although I was now a little old for Muffin's antics, I appreciated the kind gift. I was surprised one evening when Doreen and Bernard told me that we were going out and I should bring the book along. After a short ride in the car, we stopped outside a house in Chelsea and Doreen took me up to the front door and rang the bell. The door was answered by a lady that I didn't know but who turned out to be Annette Mills, the creator of Muffin the Mule and author of my book. Unknown to me, my aunt had telephoned her earlier that day to arrange for me to visit and have my book autographed. Annette took us inside and over a cup of tea she chatted to me and Doreen about her work and the TV programme. I was somewhat overwhelmed at meeting a famous person for the first time in my life and didn't say much but I treasured both the unexpected experience as well as the newly-signed book. Fortunately, my journey back home on the train was uneventful, being both swifter and warmer than the drive down in Bernard's car. A few months later, my aunt and uncle left Notting Hill. Their time there had allowed them to save enough money for a deposit on a modern detached house with a garden in the much more salubrious area of Walton on Thames.

Apart from my visits to London, I also had two week-long summer breaks in Weston Super Mare, the first with Brian and then a second time two years later when I went on my own. During these seaside visits we stayed in a large Victorian house, perched on a steep slope at the edge of the town centre that was operated by a charity providing holidays for disadvantaged children. Most of the boys there during my visits were from London but there were also a few from the Birmingham area, ranging in age from eight to fourteen. Our trips to Weston were arranged by one of my mother's clients who worked with the charity and was able to secure places for us. The alert reader will perhaps have noticed that I have avoided using the word 'holiday' so far for these visits; they were not pleasant holiday experiences as far as I was concerned. However, I suppose our absences gave my mother a respite from looking after us which was probably more important.

As might be expected, the regime in Weston was fairly strict. The house was managed by a resident warden, a kindly enough man, plus two young male assistants, a matron and a couple of kitchen staff. We slept in two large dormitories in camp beds on the top floor, with around a dozen boys in each room. Breakfast and supper were provided, served in the communal dining room but not lunch, except on Sunday. From Monday to Saturday we were expected to be out of the house by 9.30 in the morning and not return until 4pm, rain or shine. On Sundays, we were all marched down to one of the local churches in the morning, then back again for lunch and in the afternoon, we were taken to the cinema, followed by an ice-cream on the way home. After supper, there was a common room that we could all use with a few books and board games plus a wind-up gramophone with some old 78s which was a novelty for me as we didn't have a record player at home. My favourite record was *Ol' Man River* sung by Paul Robeson – a slow, rather mournful song for a youngster like me but it suited my mood. [6] Coincidentally, my mother had given me a copy of Huckleberry Finn to read during the holiday so each evening my mind was more on the Mississippi than Weston Super Mare. Some years later in April 1959, I went on a school trip to see Robeson play Othello at the Royal Shakespeare Theatre in Stratford. Although I'm sure his acting was excellent, whenever he was on stage his sonorous rendition of *Ol' Man River* just kept running through my mind.

With around twenty-five lively boys of varying ages in the house, it was inevitable that there was some arguing and scrapping between the boys with the older ones trying to establish superiority over the weaker or younger ones. Fortunately, on my first visit, I had Brian to protect me and by my second visit, I was both older and stronger, so able to look after myself. During the day, Brian and I would

---

[6] Robeson was a famous Negro singer and actor from the USA.

wander around town or the beach just trying to find something to do. If it was sunny, it was OK, we might hang around the Grand Pier or join in a game of football on the beach with other kids. However, on rainy days (and there were always several) it was hard to stay out all day. We didn't have umbrellas and there was very little shelter anywhere apart from inside the shops or in one beach hut on the promenade. But after an hour sitting on its hard, wooden benches watching the rain blow in across the bay, I began to question the value of my Weston 'holidays'. Brian and I each had sixpence a day to spend which if pooled was enough to buy some chips and a bag of sweets for lunch with a penny or two left over for the arcades on the Pier. For some reason after a couple of days, I started buying rolls of Horlicks tablets each day instead of chips for lunch. I think there were nine tablets in each roll so I could eat three during each morning and afternoon plus enjoy three for lunch. It wasn't exactly very nutritious but it kept my hunger at bay.

Towards the end of my first visit, Brian and I discovered the donkeys on the beach. There were maybe half a dozen of them, brought down each day by a couple of rather gipsy-looking men to provide rides for the children. We noticed that at busy times, the two men couldn't cope and so quickly volunteered our services to help walk the donkeys up and down the beach with the children on. Apart from a couple of tips from the parents, we didn't make any money but at least it gave us something to do. When I returned two years later, I went straight down to the beach on the first morning and was delighted to find that the donkeys were still there, together with the same two men. I hung around making myself useful helping with the rides and by the end of the day the men agreed that they would pay me one shilling for each whole day that I turned up to help. Suddenly, my one-week stay in Weston Super Mare didn't seem that much of a problem and I now had enough money to buy chips and a roll of Horlicks tablets.

Nowadays, people often say that there was more of a community spirit in the 'good old days' of the 1950s but I don't remember it like that at all. Apart from the people who shared our house, I can't recall my mother ever having much contact with any of our immediate neighbours in Kenilworth Road. I have no recollection of anything other than an occasional word being exchanged and we certainly had no meaningful social relationship or friendship with any of them. I do however, remember a big rumpus one day when I innocently climbed over the garden wall to retrieve my ball that had gone next door. No-one said anything to me at the time but apparently, the neighbour later complained so strongly to my mother that she made sure I understood I was never to do that again. When I was around seven or eight years old, I was invited for tea one day by the family that had recently moved into the large house immediately opposite us. They had two children, a boy my age, who went to the preparatory school a little further along Kenilworth Road and a girl a year or two younger. I enjoyed the tea, lots of delicious home-made cakes and biscuits and happily played with the boy in his garden for a couple of hours until it was time to go home. However, I was never invited back. I don't know if I made some social gaffe or was simply deemed unsuitable to mix with their son. Whatever the reason, we were subsequently shunned by this family; the parents never spoke to my mother and although I occasionally saw the son in the street, he was clearly under strict instructions not to talk to me. It was much the same with our other immediate neighbours. If we crossed paths in the street, they might say hello but that was the limit of any social intercourse. I suspect that the stigma of my mother being a lone parent combined with my sister's Down's syndrome were enough to put them off trying to get to know us. Probably for the same reasons, my mother never seemed to make close friends with the parents of any of my school mates.

But it wasn't just our family that experienced such social problems. I well remember occasional visits to the home of Brian's best friend, Phil. He lived in a small two-up, two-down house in Morton Street, a few hundred yards from our flat in Kenilworth Road. Morton Street was largely comprised of two rows of Victorian terraced buildings that could easily have been the setting for ITV's future soap, Coronation Street and was therefore the kind of place where, despite the evident poverty, one might think of as having a strong community spirit. However, this certainly didn't appear to be the case to me from what I saw or heard when I went round with Brian. Phil's parents seemed to be in permanent dispute with the neighbours, both next door and further down the street which on one occasion led to a brawl on the pavement outside. Perhaps because of this, Phil seemed to prefer to spend most of his free time at our house or out playing with Brian. When a teenage girl a few doors down from Phil's house became pregnant and had a baby, she was abandoned by her 'boyfriend' and both sets of parents effectively disowned her. I remember seeing the poor girl sitting on the steps outside her house in tears one afternoon, rocking her baby to and fro in a battered old pushchair. She had lost her job, couldn't work and was now an unmarried mother whose future prospects looked very bleak. I'm sure that scenes like this were to be found in any town in Britain at the time.

Although there were some charitable organizations working hard to assist the poor and disadvantaged such as housing trusts and Barnado's Homes, their reach outside the big cities was limited and they were far fewer in number than today. The National Health Service was up and running of course, as was the payment of child benefit allowances but there was little else and most of the poorer people were dependant on whatever help they could get from by family or friends. This type of support network is what might now be called the 'Big Society' but in reality, it was only a 'Little Society' in those days. People and institutions then were in general much more bigoted and narrow-minded than they are now. Neither were the local churches that most of us regularly attended particularly supportive. For example, I can't recall any effective intervention by the Leamington Catholic church to help Mrs Hussey during her many years of abuse. Also, I remember my mother telling me one evening as we walked home from church that she had been discouraged from taking communion by the vicar as she was both divorced and living as a single mother. I don't know which of these was the greater crime in the eyes of the church at that time but my mother certainly wasn't very pleased to be marginalized like that. There will always be people who through a combination of choices, circumstances and sheer bad luck, find themselves destitute or at the margins of society in great difficulty. While there may have been perhaps a gentler rhythm to life then, it seems to me that in general the situation of the poor and disabled is significantly easier now than in the late 1940s or early 1950s, as is the possibility for them to move out of poverty.

Of course we had friends, both in Leamington itself as well as further afield. In addition to my upstairs neighbour, Dennis, I had several good school friends and my mother through her dressmaking activities knew a lot of people, one or two of whom she was close to. However, her female clients were all inevitably married and my mother's single status always remained an awkward barrier to developing meaningful social relationships through these contacts. I can't recall my mother ever being invited out to any adult social gathering such as a party or visit to the theatre. Although I do remember that several of my mother's clients were extremely helpful to her during our occasional periods of crisis and were very generous with flowers on my mother's birthday or small gifts at Christmas time.

We also had visitors from time to time such as Doreen and Bernard from London or Aunt Mary and Uncle Joe who drove over to see us from their home in Galley Common near Nuneaton, usually once a year. We also stayed in touch with our former tenants, the Merricks, after they moved out and they used to pop in from time to time to see us. I always looked forward to Joe and Mary's visits, not because they were ever particularly kind to me but because my mother did her best to lay on a fine spread which I much enjoyed. The large gate-legged table in the window of our living room was opened up and covered with a fancy white lace tablecloth onto which my mother laid out a variety of sandwiches, cold cuts, fruit and cakes that she had spent the whole morning preparing. Putting on a good culinary show was obviously important for my mother – a matter of family pride for which the following week's housekeeping budget usually suffered. Because we didn't have a car and reaching Galley Common by public transport was both expensive and impractical, we never visited them. A pity really, as I am sure they would have provided an equally impressive Sunday tea.

My mother was also close friends with a couple called Joan and Andrew who initially lived in a small flat near the castle in Kenilworth and occasionally, my mother, Fiona and I would take the bus to visit them on Sunday afternoons. Andrew was tall, gangly, amiable man with a bushy, ginger beard and always smoking his pipe while Joan was dark-haired, petite and more serious. They were nice people and clearly got on well with my mother. After a while Joan and Andrew moved to a newly-built bungalow in Common Lane on the outskirts of Kenilworth and for a couple of years during the summer months I used to spend most of my Saturdays with them. Like Doreen and Bernard in London, Joan and Andrew had no children and I suppose in a way I was a surrogate child on loan for the day. They were always very kind to me and seemed genuinely happy for me to spend my Saturdays with them. Andrew was a keen gardener, which was fortunate as their new house had a very long rear garden that had to be sorted out and cultivated. At the top, Andrew laid out a large vegetable plot and most Saturdays I would spend some time with him helping to lay it out and plant it up. He set aside a small corner of the plot and gave me various seeds so that under his guidance I could experiment with growing my own salad vegetables. As we didn't have our own garden, I found this all great fun and was fascinated over the weeks to see the seeds start to sprout up above the soil and then gradually develop into radishes, carrots or lettuces. I was very proud when I took my first crop home to show my mother.

Andrew usually gave me some pocket money each Saturday afternoon and with this I would buy a few sweets and a bottle of pop such as Tizer or dandelion and burdock lemonade at the nearby grocery shop. After a while, I got to know a few of the local boys who also hung around the shop and we would often go down the road to play together on the common. This was an extensive area of sandy hillocks, largely covered in high ferns in the late summer with narrow winding paths running through it – ideal for boys to play. Our favourite game was fern fights. We would each pull up half a dozen of the larger ferns, strip off all the leaves apart from a couple at the top and then use them as small spears to throw at each other as we chased up and down the paths. It was quite harmless but good fun. Sadly, my weekly visits to Kenilworth eventually came to an end when I later took a Saturday job but we stayed in touch with Joan and Andrew and they came over to see us occasionally until we left Kenilworth Road.

In retrospect, it's strange how events that were quite minor at the time can shape one's development as a child and there were two incidents when I was with Joan and Andrew that affected me. The first was one summer afternoon, when my mother, Fiona and I went for a picnic in the gardens of Kenilworth Castle with Joan and Andrew. After we had finished eating, I went off by myself to explore the castle ruins. I was standing at the foot of part of the ramparts watching some boys of about my age walking along the top of the wall immediately above me when suddenly, one of them slipped and fell off. As he dropped down on top of me, I instinctively put out my arms to try to catch him. Although I managed to break his fall, I couldn't fully hold onto him due to the speed of his descent and his weight and we both ended up in a jumbled heap on the rocky ground below the wall. Totally unharmed, the boy then leapt up and with a quick word of thanks, rushed off to re-join his friends. I was not quite so lucky and when I stood up, I saw that not only were my knees and one of my elbows grazed and bleeding but my best white Sunday shirt was all dirty. In a bit of a daze, I wandered back to find my mother who when she saw me, asked in a rather scolding tone what on earth had I been doing to get in such a state. I hesitated, it just didn't seem worth trying to explain what had happened, that I had just saved the life of some unknown boy, or at least prevented him from being seriously injured. I knew I probably wouldn't be believed so, on reflection, it seemed much easier to simply reply that I had tripped over. With that explanation, my mother then gently cleaned my wounds and brushed the worst of the dirt from my shirt. I then understood that sometimes in life, it is easier to tell a white lie than to attempt the truth.

The second incident happened the following year. Joan was a teacher and always keen to help improve my English vocabulary and spelling by occasionally doing little tests with me that she used at school. I remember arriving for lunch one warm summer's day after a very trying journey on the bus from Leamington and describing myself as being 'buggered'. This was a word that I had picked up a few days before from one of my school friends which I thought sounded rather expressive without realizing it was then deemed to be very bad slang. As soon as I uttered the word, Andrew and Joan fell silent and I saw a look of shock and horror on Joan's face as she stared across the table at me. After a few seconds, Joan told me in a very firm tone that it was not a nice word. She added that it was almost as bad as a swear word and I shouldn't use it. I was surprised how such a seemingly innocuous word could cause such offence but resolved to be much more careful in my use of the English language in future.

Chapter Six
FAMILY ROUTINES

The Leamington of my childhood years was essentially a quiet, relatively prosperous and predominately white English middle-class town, like hundreds of others across England. The overall character and appearance of Leamington was largely established by the rapid expansion in house building during the prosperous late Georgian to mid-Victorian eras. Large detached villas and groups of fine, white or cream-stuccoed town houses, many of them laid out close to the river or in attractive squares and crescents, filled the town's central district. From the latter part of the 19th century onwards, rows of substantial detached and semi-detached brick houses had been built along tree-lined avenues. The town centre was invariably busy and although Leamington didn't have a professional theatre then, there were cinemas, parks, concerts in the imposing Royal Pump Rooms or Jephson Gardens and a range of various sporting activities. The world's first tennis club was actually established in Leamington in 1872 and the rules of modern lawn tennis were drawn up there.

From its inception as a fashionable spa town, Leamington had consistently attracted the rich and famous as visitors and residents, both from elsewhere in Britain and overseas. The Prince Regent and his sister Princess Augusta, Queen Adelaide, John Nash and the Duke of Wellington all came to try the spa waters. Prince Louis Napoléon Bonaparte, the exiled nephew of Napoléon Bonaparte arrived in Leamington in 1838 and stayed for almost a year before returning to France to eventually become Emperor Bonaparte III. The then Princess Victoria visited the town in 1830 and returned again as Queen in 1858. As a special mark of her favour in

1838 she authorized the town to style itself Royal Leamington Spa. This influx of famous and influential people gave Leamington a more cosmopolitan atmosphere than might otherwise have been expected for such a provincial town. Of course, there were many poor people in the town, mostly living in dilapidated Victorian slum tenements or in run-down, converted flats in some of the then un-loved large town houses. A few rows of compact 'pre-fab' houses, built as temporary homes immediately after the War on the edge of the Campion Hills, were also still in use. But by the mid-1950s, Leamington was in the middle of a major expansion of its housing stock. Extensive council estates were being constructed at both ends of the town and some of the worst slum buildings were ear-marked for demolition.

The late 1940s and early 1950s were still a period of austerity following the hardships of the wartime restrictions and rationing existed until 1954. However, consumer goods were gradually becoming more accessible to everyone, local industry was expanding and employment was easy to find. The growth in the demand for labour saw increasing numbers of immigrants arrive in the town, especially from Ireland and Italy but they had little adverse impact on Leamington's genteel character. There were occasional mutterings in the town about the immigrant problem but it never seemed to amount to much and both these groups of new arrivals generally quickly merged into Leamington's society. The Irish swelled attendances at the local Catholic church as well as a few pubs while the Italians steadily expanded our choice of cafes and restaurants. There was only a handful of Asian and black families resident in the town at the time; they were a rare sight on the streets and there were none at either of my schools. As far as I can recall, apart from once visiting the only Chinese restaurant in town with my mother when I was sixteen, I didn't meet a single person of Asian or African origin until I went to university in 1964.

There was however, one notable black family in Leamington that became nationally famous, the Turpins. Dick Turpin and his younger brother Randolph, were the sons of Lionel Turpin from British Guiana who had settled in Leamington with his white British wife and they both became internationally successful boxers. Dick was the British and Commonwealth middleweight champion in the late 1940s and reputedly the first black fighter to win a British boxing title. Randolph, who turned professional at eighteen in 1946 was trained by his elder brother at the boys club in Leamington. Known as the 'Leamington Licker', Randolph went on to take British, European and Commonwealth titles and in 1951 he defeated the American, Sugar Ray Robinson to take the world middleweight title, becoming an overnight national hero. Sadly, his success didn't last long; he steadily lost all his titles and found it hard to adjust to his lack of celebrity status. After being declared bankrupt in the 1960s, Turpin committed suicide by shooting himself in 1966 at his home in Leamington where he lived with his wife and four daughters.

While talking of famous old Leamingtonians, I should also mention Sir Frank Whittle who is credited with the invention of the turbojet engine which was first patented in 1930. Although born in Coventry, Whittle moved to Leamington at the age of nine with his family during the First World War. Frank was educated at Milverton Road Junior School and Leamington College for Boys, the two schools that I subsequently attended, though sadly, I never matched his achievements. However, when in the sixth form, I was lucky enough to win the annual geography prize which was presented to me at speech day by the great man himself.

Like most households in Britain at the time, we had a well-defined family routine. The majority of people worked at least a five-and-a-half-day week and my mother was no exception. The only difference for her was that all the household duties such as cleaning, washing and shopping had to be fitted into her Monday through Saturday dressmaking schedule. Mondays in our Leamington flat were typically wash-days. This labour-intensive process was a far cry from the relative ease of today's electric washing machines and spin driers. Our dirty clothes were first boiled up in a large pan on the kitchen stove for an hour or so. Since there could be as many as four or five of us living in the flat at times, there could be several pans boiling away which usually resulted in the kitchen becoming completely filled with a malodorous steam. Any particularly soiled items were given individual treatment over the sink on a scrubbing board with a hard block of yellow soap before being into the pan to boil. Once they were deemed clean enough, the clothes were taken to the bathroom where they were then passed through a hand-operated mangle, with the squeezed-out water draining away into the bath. The final stage in this cleaning process was to carry everything downstairs in baskets to be hung out to dry and air in the back yard. At the end of the day, everything had to be then hauled back upstairs for ironing. It was hard physical work and although Brian, Pat or I were sometimes around to help, most of the effort fell on my mother's shoulders and she was invariably completely worn out on Monday nights.

My mother usually did her main household shopping on Saturday mornings and apart from the brief period when Gran was living with us, my sister and I always went with her as she couldn't leave us alone in the flat. The three of us would walk down Kenilworth Road and on down The Parade which was Leamington's main shopping street. The town's retail trade had recovered quickly after the War and by the early 1950s, it boasted a wide range of both department stores and independent shops as well as the ubiquitous Woolworths and Marks & Spencer. Among the larger independent shops were Bobby's at the lower end of The Parade selling very fashionable clothing, Francis's, an exclusive shop around the corner in Bath

Street and Woodward's, a large clothing and haberdashery store. My favourite was the department store of Burgis & Colbourne (now a House of Fraser store) which had been founded as a family business in the Victorian era and was then Leamington's largest retail business. In my day, the store offered a particularly wide range of merchandise and goods but it was their large food hall and delicatessen that I found most interesting.

I loved wandering around the different counters looking at the fascinating variety of produce. The arrays of Continental-style bread, salami and cooked meats or stands of exotic cheeses were mostly beyond our budget but occasionally, my mother, unable to resist the temptations, would splash out and buy a small treat for lunch. Her favourite was the Italian Mortadella salami, a speciality of Bologna flavoured with pork fat and pistachios which she would buy to eat with a fresh French baguette. However, for a really special treat, another Leamington icon of the time, Elizabeth's cake shop, located on the upper part of The Parade took pride of place in my mind. In the words of today's *Mr Kipling*, her cakes were 'exceedingly good' and the shop was well known in the area. On the odd occasions when my mother had a really good week with her dressmaking, we would call into Elizabeth's on the way back from town and buy a couple of cakes. My favourites were her delicious meringues filled with fresh cream but my mother always went for the blackcurrant tarts, also topped with fresh cream. We couldn't wait to get home to devour them.

Looking back now, it is intriguing that there was such a wide gamut of continental produce available in Burgis & Colbourne's delicatessen in the early 1950s. I don't know if this was a reflection of the numbers and tastes of the town's post-war immigrant population or simply the cosmopolitan food preferences of Leamingtonians in general. But clearly, the store wouldn't have stocked these items if they hadn't sold. We tend to think of the delicatessen as being a more modern arrival on the British shopping scene, at least outside London. However, this shows that even then, for those who had the money, there was a wider choice of food available than the traditional British fare. It's perhaps even more remarkable considering the fact that the remnants of the rationing system introduced during the War were still in effect then and we each had a ratio book with coupons inside, grey for my mother and blue for Fiona and me. Of most concern to me was the rationing of sweets which lasted into 1953 and until then, we were only allowed 2oz. each week. The last remaining elements of rationing didn't end until July 1954, when restrictions on the sale and purchase of meat and bacon were finally lifted.

Of course, in those days there were no supermarkets and so our weekly shop was mostly a series of separate visits to the butcher, grocer, greengrocer and baker. Normally, these trips were without incident; my mother would set off along the street going from shop to shop, firmly gripping the hand of my sister, Fiona. I would traipse along somewhere behind and then once in the shop, would take over the job of supervising Fiona. One day, while my mother was queuing to buy some fruit in our usual greengrocer's, I failed to notice that Fiona had edged up to the man in front of us in the queue. A few moments later the man emitted a loud gasp and swivelled round with a bright red face to stare at Fiona and me. Unseen by me, Fiona had apparently reached forward between the man's legs and grabbed his penis, provoking the understandably shocked response from the man. Of course, we didn't know exactly what had happened until the ravaged man in the quietest of whispers explained to my mother the reason for his outburst. It was all highly embarrassing, both for the man and my mother and she apologised profusely, also in the lowest of voices. Once back out in the street, my mother initially vented her anger and humiliation at this incident on me – I hadn't looked after my sister properly - but that soon subsided and we walked home in a fit of giggles. What had possessed Fiona to act in this strange manner in the greengrocer's was beyond us. As far as either of us knew, she had never exhibited any interest in the male (or female) anatomy before or indeed since. It was just one of those curious incidents that make life unpredictable and as a result, all the more interesting.

Once I was old enough, I was occasionally dispatched by my mother to do the odd bit of shopping on my own, either for food or for urgent supplies from Woodward's for her dressmaking work. As a ten-year-old boy, I would often get strange looks from the young female shop assistants in the haberdashery department when I stood there and asked for a twelve inch blue zip or several yards of material or braid. But no-one ever queried why I wanted such things and once I had handed over the cash, they were always duly wrapped up in a brown paper parcel for me to carry home. One afternoon after I had come home from school, I was sent to the nearest corner shop at the end of our street with a silver shilling coin (5p in today's money) to buy some bread rolls and eggs. When I arrived at the shop and reached into my trouser pocket for the money, I found it was no longer there. Instead, I discovered a small hole in the lining and realized that the coin must have dropped out somewhere en route. I desperately retraced my steps back up the street to try to find my shilling but in vain. In trepidation, I returned to our flat and reported the unfortunate loss to my mother. After I had been admonished for being so careless, the two of us went out into the street to search again for the lost coin but it was nowhere to be seen. My mother was both annoyed and visibly upset as she explained to me that apart from a few coppers in her purse, it was the only cash she had. I was sent to bed early, annoyed at what had happened but also hungry as I had no tea. When I put my shorts on the next morning, I noticed that the hole in my pocket had been carefully repaired by my mother overnight.

On Sundays, we invariably went to church which for the first few years meant Sunday school for me in the mornings and then returning with my mother for the evening service. Not only was general church attendance higher then but religious festivals were also much more important such as Advent and Palm Sunday. Good Friday was a holiday for most people and the majority of shops closed for the afternoon. In the summer-time, Sunday afternoons were usually set aside for visits to either Jephson Gardens or Victoria Park which lead off at right angles on each side of the lower end of The Parade, enclosing the riverside like a familiar, old green scarf. As described earlier, when Gran was with us, we all walked down to one of the parks pushing Gran in her wheelchair. Later, when Gran wasn't with us, my mother would usually ride her old, sit-up-and-beg bike down to the park with Fiona in a child's seat on the back, our picnic in a basket on the front and me cycling alongside. Most of the time, we would head to the bandstand and find a spot to settle down to listen to the music and enjoy our picnic. These free Sunday afternoon concerts were popular with hundreds of people gathered all around the bandstand on the benches or the grass. There really wasn't much else to do with virtually everything closed on Sundays and since transistor radios hadn't yet arrived from the USA, young people had no alternative for listening to music outdoors. Not that Fiona or I were terribly interested in the band music, we were just happy to run around and play among the crowds. My lingering memories are of making daisy chains and searching in vain through the park for the fabled four-leafed clover or simply lying stretched out in the sun on the newly-cut grass, breathing in its pungent, bitter-sweet aroma.

If the weather was particularly warm, we would spend the afternoon at the children's paddling pool at the far end of Victoria Park where Fiona and I would splash around while my mother sat quietly reading. At going-home time, there was usually a clamour for an ice cream from both of us; sometimes our wish was granted, sometimes not. We rarely went to the town's parks during winter; it was cold, there were no bands playing and no ice creams. However, when we did, it was either to see the fascinating and sometimes dramatic ice structures that covered the ponds and fountains after a particularly cold snap or to marvel at the power of the normally sedate River Leam flowing in full spate through the parks. The river used to flood quite regularly, normally just overflowing its banks and filling up adjacent fields but periodically, the flooding was much more serious with parts of the lower town going under water. When the floods occurred during the depth of winter, the flooded fields froze over and proved popular with local residents for ice skating.

For some reason that I have never fully understood, we didn't pay much attention to birthdays at home. My mother always bought me or my sister a card and usually a small present, as well as one for Gran, Brian or Pat when they were living with us. Later on, once I was old enough to receive pocket money, I would also buy a present for my mother and after my father's visit, he started sending me birthday cards from Canada. But while we were at Kenilworth Road I can't recall any of us having special celebrations with candle-topped cakes or parties with friends. Although I went to my own friends' birthday parties at their houses, I didn't have my own birthday party until I was fourteen when I invited three school friends home for tea. Undoubtedly our family situation was a contributory factor in this. Money was tight, my mother worked extremely hard with little spare time to prepare something special and when there was only the three of us, it probably didn't seem worth making a lot of effort.

I think however, it went deeper than that. As far as I could gather, my mother's own upbringing was difficult and disjointed. She was an only child and lived with her father for much of her life. I never knew what happened to her mother as the subject of her wider family never seemed to be discussed, either by my mother or Gran. Since my mother's father was a travelling salesman, they moved around a lot living in a variety of digs and hotels.

Although he was apparently a good father, this life-style inevitably resulted in little contact with other family members and made it impossible for my mother to make any lasting childhood friendships. With just the two of them, it probably didn't seem worth making a fuss and that attitude probably carried over into my mother's adult life. Her quiet, reserved personality as an adult probably derived from this itinerant and restricted upbringing as well as her diffident attitude towards birthdays.

Christmas however, was different in various ways and was always celebrated as best as we could manage. It was a naturally jolly time throughout the country and was therefore hard to avoid or overlook. The fact that many of my mother's regular clients would send us Christmas cards and some also called in with gifts made the festivities hard to ignore. One lady called Mrs Jefferson I think, who lived in Leamington's exclusive Northumberland Avenue always tipped my mother and brought packets of preserved dates or candied fruit for me and some sweets for Fiona. Other clients might bring a box of chocolates or a tin of biscuits and on Christmas Eve, the lady who had a farm would often appear with a chicken for us to roast the next day. We always had a small Christmas tree in the living room, decorated with a gold star on top, lots of tinsel and later on, a set of electric lights, at least when they worked. My mother used to make up a stocking for each of us containing our presents, an orange and a few sweets or peanuts in their shells. We always opened our stockings early on Christmas morning in my mother's bedroom which was the closest we came to having any kind of family tradition at Christmas. I think my mother's peripatetic childhood meant that she and her father never developed any sense of Yule-Tide or family traditions generally. Fiona rarely took any interest in her presents or orange, Christmas for her was all about sweets – the more the merrier.

One year when we were small, Fiona and I were given tickets to an afternoon Christmas party in the town hall that was organized for the poorer and disadvantaged children of Leamington. It turned out to be a noisy and rather chaotic event with several dozen kids excitedly shouting and running around the ornate and normally tranquil town hall building, much to the consternation of those trying to control things. Despite the general chaos, there were party games plus a good tea and at the end, we were all given a small parcel by Father Christmas. I don't know whether the town council ever decided to repeat this event but if they did, we certainly weren't invited.

My father used to regularly send me a Christmas card together with a small money order, half of which would go into the family 'pot' and the rest for me to spend. However, that first Christmas after his visit, he also ordered a stamp album for me from Stanley Gibbons in London together with a large starter pack of world stamps. The album was an A4-sized, spiral bound, beginner's worldwide album with pages printed for each country displaying a picture of its national flag. My father was an enthusiastic philatelist and obviously felt I might enjoy starting a stamp collection of my own. He was right and over the years not only did my little collection steadily grow but I also gradually learned something about many of the countries, their location in the world, their capital city, local currency and so on. My subsequent interest in geography (which I later studied at university) probably stemmed from these small, stamp collecting beginnings.

For several years, my grandmother in Toronto usually sent a small gift parcel as well. Mostly, this would contain a box of some form of fancy sweets or Canadian candy. Opening and consuming the contents of these presents on Christmas morning was always looked forward to and enjoyed. One Christmas, an intriguing, much larger package arrived which frustratingly remained in my mother's bedroom for a couple of weeks until I was allowed to open it on Christmas morning. It turned out to be a junior baseball bat together with a stitched, white leather ball and a catcher's glove. What a great present for a nine-year-old boy. Although I had no idea how to play baseball, I didn't need lessons on how to use a bat and ball and had great fun with my new present in the back alley and later in the park. Eventually, I lost the ball and glove somehow but the bat stayed with me for many years. Although my grandmother's presents dried up when I reached my early teens, she did not forget me and on my twenty-first birthday she thoughtfully sent me a silver cigarette case that had belonged to my Uncle Rod. It was engraved with his initials and my grandmother had kept it as a memento of her dead son all these years. Although it was sent by registered mail, it never arrived and despite months of enquiries with Royal Mail they said they were unable to trace it.

The Christmas after Uncle Stan and Aunt Laurie's extended stay with us by, we received a large box that had been sent from New Zealand. When we opened it, we found it was full of half-pound packets of New Zealand butter – there must have been at least a dozen in the box. My mother initially just sat and stared at the box and its contents but then she burst into a mixture of tears and smiles at the same time. She was obviously both delighted and touched by the kind thought behind this important gift. I was less impressed at first but eventually I too saw the benefit of this present from faraway New Zealand. Butter was a luxury for us and now we had enough luxury to last the family through many, many weeks. After that first shipment, we continued to receive a box of butter each Christmas for quite a few years (until Uncle Stan died I think) and our annual appreciation never diminished.

**Wynne & Bill Heather,
Lansdowne Crescent,
1943**

**Wynne & Rod,
Leamington, 1945**

Uncle Rod, (far right) 1943

11 Kenilworth Road

Father & son, Toronto

Eaton's Store, Toronto, 1947

Brian, Fiona & Rod, Victoria Park, 1952

Pat, Fiona, Gran & Rod, Victoria Park

Mrs Mitchell
& Isobel

Joan, Andrew & Rod,
Kenilworth

Chapter Seven
BOYS WILL BE BOYS

After the Merricks moved out of the upstairs flat, taking their TV with them, we were once more reduced to listening to the radio for our primary source of external entertainment. I did however, have an alternative, especially on cold or rainy days when I couldn't go outside to play. Sometimes, I would sit at the large window that looked out from our living room onto Kenilworth Road and watch the world gently go by. I remember the rag and bone man who periodically worked our road with his mangy horse and dilapidated cart. He used to announce his presence with a loud shout of 'Old rags, any old rags' that echoed up and down the street outside. Even if he was still around today, his voice just wouldn't be heard over the constant thrum of traffic. Perhaps the most noticeable difference between Leamington in the 1950s and today is the much greater volume of vehicles on the roads and the resultant ambient noise and pollution levels. Although as a main thoroughfare, Kenilworth Road was busy in the daytime, it carried nothing like the amount of traffic that it does today. In particular, the number of commercial vans and heavy goods vehicles was far, far less. When we lived there, it was easy to cross the road at any time and the side streets where I could peacefully run around are now crammed with cars parked on both sides of the road.

The rag and bone man also had a set of grinding wheels mounted on his cart and whenever we heard him in the road, my mother would dash out and get him to sharpen all her dressmaking scissors. Other images that have remained fixed in my memory are a man walking past on a breezy, rainy afternoon valiantly hanging onto his umbrella which had blown inside out; an old Foden steam roller laying new tarmac along the road with clouds of smoke pouring out of its chimney as it clanked and puffed its way backwards and forwards; the broken-down car being slowly pushed along by two men frantically trying to retain their footing in the pouring rain and the stillness of the scene during a heavy winter snow storm as large swirling snowflakes tumbled down blending the roads and pavements into a single whole. It was as if a long, white carpet was being rolled out all the way down Kenilworth Road.

Although we now had no television, I think my mother had caught the bug and when it was announced that the forthcoming coronation of Queen Elizabeth II would be shown on TV, my mother decided we should have one, ordered of course 'on tic'. It arrived the day before the great event and a man in white overalls came around to set it up for us in our living room. On the actual day, we all gathered proudly round our new acquisition and were joined for the occasion by the Mitchells and the Hussey family. My mother prepared tea and cakes which we ate from our laps while glued to the moving pictures in front of us. Although it was hard to see some of the detail at times on the tiny black and white screen, everyone was excited at being able to watch this momentous and historic event. From that day on, the TV became an important daily fixture in our lives, as it increasingly did for millions of others in Britain. BBC remained the only channel available until ITV started broadcasting in the Midlands in February 1956. For some reason, we couldn't get an ITV signal in our flat so I used to occasionally go to one of my friends in the evenings to watch commercial TV – Dragnet, an imported US police programme was my favourite then.

Around the same time, we gained access to another modern convenience, when Mrs Mitchell had a pay phone installed in the main hall on the ground floor for us all to share. Whilst it was great to now have access to a telephone, we soon found out there was a problem with this payphone installation in the hall. When someone tried to call us or the Husseys there was no-one to hand to answer it. It was difficult for the Mitchells to hear the phone ringing from their living room at the rear of the house and even if they did, they knew it wasn't usually for them and so let it ring. If we were expecting a call, we had to keep our ears open and then when it rang, we had to dash down two flights of stairs to try to pick up the receiver before the caller rang off. This process certainly improved our overall fitness and my mother had to remember to tell anyone she thought might telephone to be patient and wait for the telephone to be answered. If the call was for the Husseys, we had to either take the caller's number or get them to call back as it simply took too long to go all the way up to the top flat, find out if someone was in and for them to then go downstairs to answer the phone.

Inside our flat, my principle play area was basically a wooden desk that normally sat against one wall of our living room. Someone had given it to us when we first moved to Kenilworth Road and it had two rounded plywood ends joined across the middle by a cork-covered worktop. Because I mostly shared my mother's bedroom, my own personal space was important to me and this was where I kept all my toys, comics, small stamp collection and other boyhood bits and pieces. It also served as a play-space in that when emptied out and laid on its back, I could sit inside the central space on a cushion and make believe I was in a ship, a car or even an aeroplane. If Dennis or one of my other friends was round to play, there was just enough room for two of us to squeeze in side by side and give full reign to our imaginations. However, when it wasn't raining or too cold, I much preferred to be playing in the local streets and parks outside.

Dennis and I got up to all sorts of other stupid mischief while living at Kenilworth Road and as an adult I now feel embarrassed to describe some of these activities. Cherry-knocking (ringing someone's doorbell and then running off before they came to the door) was a game I learnt from

Dennis and was one of our regular pass-times. Another game we played for a while, was to crouch behind the garden wall at the front of our house and throw small lumps of dirt at the back of cars as they drove along the road. Because there was so much less traffic then, it was easy to pick out an approaching target vehicle and then try to hit it as it went by. This game came to an end when one of the cars we had hit, suddenly stopped and the driver got out and ran back down the road towards us. I assume he must have glimpsed our heads above the wall as he drove by and grasped what had happened. Having been discovered, Dennis and I then realized our predicament – we were stuck in our front garden with no safe escape route. If we ran back into the house the man would know where we lived and would probably ring the bell and tell my mother what we had been doing. The only alternative was to quickly dodge out from behind the wall and try to out-run the man down Kenilworth Road. We glanced at each other and simultaneously reached the same conclusion, we ran as fast as our little legs would vary us. Initially, the man chased after us but by the time we reached the corner I think he decided it was no longer worth trying to catch us and strode angrily back to his car. We didn't play that particular game again.

The approach of November 5th and Bonfire Night was something Dennis and I always looked forward to. Since we were banned from the garden at Kenilworth Road, we had no way of having a bonfire but we could still enjoy a few fireworks in the back alleyway. Each Saturday for the two or three weeks leading up to November 5th, Dennis and I would pool our financial resources and wander down to the local shop to buy a few fireworks. As there were no age restrictions on the purchase of fireworks in those days, we could buy what we wanted. Our preferences were the penny bangers and jumping jacks. We tried to be inventive in our use of our limited supplies and experimented with various ideas. Our favourite was to put bangers or jumping jacks in an empty dustbin which greatly increased the noise effects. We also tried bangers in glass jars to see if they would shatter and placed bangers in the crevices of the alleyway brick walls to amplify the explosive effect. It may just be a quirk of my imagination but the fireworks we bought then definitely seemed to be more powerful than those available today. Occasionally, one or two of the neighbours whose back yards gave onto the alley complained about the noise we made. If we were really feeling mischievous, our revenge was to light the touch paper of a jumping jack and using a long stick, push it under the yard door into their garden before running off as fast as we could.

Mounted on the landing wall at the top of the main stairs was an impressively large, gilt-framed oil painting of a biblical scene – Delilah holding up Samson's bloody head I think. This dramatic and forbidding picture was surrounded by several other smaller oils and water colours plus an extensive display of swords, daggers and other miscellaneous armaments. This whole collection, no doubt of some considerable value, belonged to the owner of the house who for some strange reason had not removed them when it was rented out. Although Dennis and I had no interest whatsoever in the paintings, the various arms were just too tempting. Initially, we just temporarily took down a couple of the knives from the wall and played with them right there in the hall. For an hour or so, in our young imaginations, we were Anglo-Saxon warriors, Red Indian braves or members of Robin Hood's gang. Once we had enough, our weapons were carefully replaced into their mountings on the wall. As time went by and nothing was said by any of the adults in the house, each weekend we gradually became bolder in both our weapon selections and where we used them. Over the course of several months, we went through the complete gamut of this wall-mounted armoury - swords, bayonets, pikes, daggers, helmets and chain-mail – creating a wonderful world of make-believe role-playing. We became knights of old, soldiers in the British Army or two of the three musketeers and eventually we dared to play in the street outside. With increased use, some of the wall-mountings failed so we simply stacked up our used weapons against the wall after playing with them but still nothing was said. For two young boys, this was a marvellous treasure-trove and it kept us both out of other mischief for months.

All good things come to an end however and we met our Waterloo one afternoon during the summer holidays in the street behind our house. For a week or so, Dennis and I had been feuding with a gang of boys from a few streets away. They had been pushing into our territory and we didn't like it but as a couple of them were in their early teens and much bigger than us, we couldn't chase them off. Then the solution came to us. On the afternoon in question, we were out in the street playing when we saw the gang approaching. We pretended to be scared and started slowly retreating back up the street and shouting for them to come and get us if they dared. They took the bait and followed us until we reached the point where our back alley met the street. Dennis and I quickly ducked around the corner and each grabbed a sword and dagger that we had placed there earlier in readiness for just this event. We rushed back out into the street, brandishing our weapons and charged at the other boys, shouting at the top of our lungs. For a brief, tense moment, it looked as if our plan wasn't going to work but then suddenly, the enemy broke ranks, turned and fled down the street. We followed them for a while until we were sure they weren't coming back and then headed for home, exhilarated by our easy victory. As we regained our alley all breathless and excited, my mother suddenly appeared, heading out to the corner shop and we all but bumped into each other. She was understandably shocked to see us so flush-faced and carrying swords. Within seconds, under her severe questioning, our erstwhile bravado collapsed and the truth came out. We were confined to the house for the rest of the day and banned from ever touching the weapons in the hall ever again. An instruction that we thenceforth followed, well more or less.

Along with thousands of other boys across the country, the end of the summer holidays and arrival of early autumn meant only one thing, it was scrumping time. According to the Oxford Dictionary, this peculiarly English verb derives from the mid-19th century word of *scrump*, meaning a withered apple. Somewhere along the line, the word has become a verb that described the nefarious activity of helping oneself to fruit from the trees in other people's gardens. I never gave any thought to the origin of the word but I certainly wasn't interested in taking withered apples. I only wanted the ripe, ready-to-eat ones and Dennis and I knew exactly where to go to find the best fruit as the various trees ripened. Usually it was easy as many fruit trees had branches overhanging or alongside their respective boundary walls or fences. We could simply reach up and help ourselves to the low-hanging fruit or knock it down with sticks. But as lots of local kids were raiding the same trees, the easy fruit soon disappeared and we had to be more adventurous. Generally, this involved one of us climbing up onto the brick wall, stretching out to reach the fruit inside the garden and then dropping it down to one's accomplice. This method was more dangerous because someone could easily come by and catch you up on the wall or a vigilant owner might come out and try to chase you. In these situations, whoever was on the wall was most at risk as he had only seconds to clamber down and try to escape down the street. Neither Dennis nor I were ever caught scrumping and although we did have some very close calls, it was all part of the fun.

Although I learnt to read when I was four or five years old, I was never an avid reader as a child, unlike my mother for whom reading was her main form of relaxation when she had time. The occasional literary Christmas present such as Robinson Crusoe and Wind in the Willows largely remained on the bedroom shelf only partly read and I didn't become seriously interested in reading books until I was fourteen or fifteen. Somehow, sitting quietly to read a book didn't suit me and I much preferred to be out playing with my friends. However, like most boys of my age at that time, I was a keen reader of comics which sold by the million every week in the 1950s. My favourite was *The Eagle* with its stories of Dan Dare, 'the pilot of the future' but *The Beano* and *The Dandy* were good substitutes although I never had the money to buy any of them regularly. One Saturday afternoon, my mother sent me off to deliver a dress that she had altered to a large house off the Warwick Road. When the lady of the house answered the door, I collected the money she owed and as I was leaving she asked me if I liked comics. It seemed a strange question but when I said yes, she beckoned me inside the house and led me to a room upstairs. After she opened the door to what was obviously an office, I could see stacks of various comics lying around in piles on the floor; the room was full of them. She asked me if I would like to take a few and if so to help myself. I hesitated initially but she encouraged me forwards explaining that her husband was a writer for the publisher of these comics and always had plenty of copies. Quickly recovering from my amazement at seeing so many comics in one place, I selected as many as I thought it reasonable to take and after expressing my sincere thanks, I headed home. After that, I made sure my mother knew that I wanted to personally deliver any other work for this address and I was lucky enough to be able to subsequently top up my comic reading several times.

By the time I was ten, delivering my mother's finished dress-making output on my bike was part of my regular routine, both in the evenings and at weekends. Although it was a chore, I knew it was one of the few ways in which I could directly help her. The task of cycling around town in all weathers was, however, relieved by the small tips that I occasionally received from some of my mother's clients. I soon got to know those who tipped and those who didn't and adjusted my willingness to deliver the various packages accordingly. If the delivery was for a good tipper, I was almost always instantly available but if it wasn't, then I would try to find any excuse to delay my departure. I wasn't always able to collect the money due when I made a delivery. Sometimes the clients were out and if their husbands answered the door, they weren't always keen to pay for their wife's things. On other occasions, the client would promise to drop the money round to my mother later in the week. These situations were very frustrating all round as we usually needed the money to live on as well as to cover what my mother had already paid out for the material etc. In addition, of course I didn't receive any tips.

As I didn't have a carrier or basket on my bike, carrying the larger parcels was sometimes difficult, especially if it was very windy or raining. With the parcel tucked under one arm, I had to steer, brake and change gear with just one hand and several times I had near escapes. Once I crashed into the back of a car that had pulled up sharply at traffic lights and went straight over my handlebars landing spread-eagled on the car boot with my face pushed up against the rear window. On another occasion, I lost my balance while weaving through traffic in town and ended up flat on the road in front of an oncoming bus which fortunately managed to stop inches from my face. Unsurprisingly, the bus driver's comments out of his window were less than complimentary about my cycling skills. On one particularly wet winter's day, the brown paper bag I was carrying got soaked and eventually the dress inside slipped out and dropped onto the street as I was cycling along. I immediately pulled up and retrieved the previously neatly ironed and folded dress was now a soaking wet heap and had several dirty smudges on it. I did my best to wrap it up again and when I reached the client's home, I quickly handed over the sodden package with a brief apologetic explanation of what had happened. The lady seemed quite understanding and taking the parcel from me, thanked me for delivering it. As I cycled off, I dreaded to think what her reaction would be once she opened it up and saw the state her dress was in but I never heard any more about it.

Chapter Eight
FOOD, GLORIOUS FOOD

We must have been a relatively healthy family. Of course, we all had the inevitable bouts of winter colds which sometimes badly affected my mother but I can't remember any of us being really ill and we certainly never went to visit the doctor's surgery. The only times I saw our doctor was once when my cousin Brian, shot me in the leg with an air pistol (see page 113) and on a couple of occasions when my grandmother needed treatment. In those days, the doctor invariably came to see the patient. Perhaps we were lucky but I think at that time, most people largely took care of themselves unless seriously ill. My mother's generation had grown up before the arrival of the National Health when medical care had to be paid for and so they often retained a reluctance to call out the doctor. Aches and pains, coughs and fevers, stiff joints and backache were simply endured or hopefully eased with something from the local chemist. No-one had allergies, few people were overweight and hip or knee replacements were unheard of.

If we were fortunate in having good health and rarely seeing the doctor, our dental experiences were the complete opposite. For a couple of years, we went to a dental practice on the ground floor of one of the fancy Victorian villas in Clarendon Road. Whilst the building may have been impressive, the work of our dentist most certainly was not. Whenever I went, whether for a filling or simply an inspection, it proved to be an unpleasant and often painful experience. Not only did our dentist suffer from extreme halitosis but he frequently seemed careless in the use of his instruments, jabbing my gums with his probe or failing to find the right spot for an injection and having to repeat the process. This torture experience was finally completed by the old type of jaw juddering electric drill then in use by the dental profession. It was bad enough for my mother and me but in Fiona's case, it was a lost cause. On her first visit, my mother and I had to literally hold my screaming sister down in the chair while our clumsy dentist tried to carry out his initial inspection. Despite giving her gas to then carry out a filling, I don't think Fiona was totally unconscious. She was hysterical on the way home and after that, it became impossible to persuade her to return. Eventually, my mother decided that enough was enough and mercifully found another dentist. A year or so later, there was a report in the local paper that said our dentist had been struck off for malpractice and drunkenness. This news was of little consolation to me and my Clarendon Road experiences left me with an enduring fear of the dentist's chair.

Our diet was undoubtedly much simpler and plainer than that of most families in Britain today but as it was virtually all home-cooked, it was mostly healthy and nutritious. As long as my mother had earned enough money that week, she would go out on Saturday to buy a small joint of meat (generally a leg of New Zealand lamb). This was then roasted on Sunday for lunch, served with potatoes, a vegetable and the excellent Yorkshire puddings that my mother used to make. Pudding was usually a freshly baked fruit pie or some type of steamed pudding. My mother was a reasonable cook (when she had time) always made an effort to ensure we had a decent meal on Sunday. While lunch was being prepared and during the meal itself, we invariably listened to the BBC Light programme on the radio. Like millions of others in Britain at the time we always tuned into *Two-Way Family Favourites*, hosted by Jean Metcalf in London and Cliff Michelmore in Germany. This extremely popular programme played record requests, linking families in Britain with their loved ones in the Armed Forces, initially in Germany and later with other bases such as Cyprus.

Although unknown to the audiences at the time, Metcalf and Michelmore were building their own relationship over the airwaves and eventually married each other some years later. Other favourites were comedy programmes such as *The Navy Lark* and *The Goon Show*, although I have to admit that much of the latter went over my head.

The leftovers of the Sunday joint would gradually reappear in some form or other as the week progressed, either as cold cuts, a shepherd's pie or in a stew with dumplings. Later in the week, our main meals would generally be based around tinned spam, corned beef or pilchards with potatoes or bubble and squeak (potatoes mashed with cabbage and fried) and on Fridays, some kind of fish almost always filled the bill of fare. Our meals on Saturdays were always the most varied, being heavily dependent on the state of our household finances. Apart from more ordinary items like ham, liver or hotpot, my mother also sometimes served up pig's trotters or tripe (both of which I hated but they were favourites of my Gran) and on special occasions, home-made spaghetti using the recipe she had learnt from our former Italian tenants. In the summer months, there might be fresh fruit to follow with tinned peaches or pears in the winter.

Breakfast for me was always cereal or porridge during the winter months with maybe an occasional boiled egg and toast at weekends. Tea was usually some form of sandwich with an apple or orange if there were any and occasionally, drop scones that my mother made on an old black griddle. Sliced white bread was always an important part of our calorie intake, at least for Brian and me, being eaten both at mealtimes as well as a snack. All our meals were taken in our small kitchen, apart from the rare high teas in the living room when we had visitors or if making toast and dripping in front of the winter fire.

Common items today such as chicken and fresh salmon were a rarity in those days, at least for us. One of my mother's clients owned a farm and occasionally, when she came to collect her items, she would bring us a plucked, whole chicken or some freshly-laid eggs – a much appreciated treat during the period of rationing. I didn't have fresh salmon until I was around fifteen when I was staying in the Cotswolds with the family of one of my mother's friends and taken out for dinner. This was the first time I had been to a proper restaurant and faced with an extensive menu, I was unsure what to choose. However, when the person sitting next to me ordered poached salmon, I quickly decided to follow suit and give it a try. Served with a rich Hollandaise sauce (another new experience for me), it turned out to be delicious, although I had trouble using the fish knife and dealing with the small, fine bones which no-one had warned me about. The fact that I can still easily recall my meals after all these years is not an indication of good memory, rather it is a reflection of the basic and consistent nature of our food. Other than spaghetti, it was all pretty standard fare that provided enough calories and vitamins to keep us going. The free daily bottle of milk during the morning break at school was also an important top-up to my diet, especially in the early years when meat, cheese and eggs were rationed.

There were however, occasions when the established routine didn't function, usually when my mother was ill and unable to earn any money. Although she generally had good health, at least until her last few years when she was diagnosed with breast cancer, she did suffer from the occasional heavy cold or flu. Although these bouts of sickness usually passed within a few days, there were times when she had an extremely bad dose and was confined to bed for a week or so. As she was then not able to complete whatever dress-making work she had on hand, she had no income. Since she was rarely able to put anything by for the proverbial 'rainy day', it meant we had to survive on whatever money she had in her purse the day she became ill and whatever limited amount of food was already in the house. On such occasions, I can remember going to the local shop to buy a couple of bread rolls that we ate with a can of Italian plum tomatoes or my own culinary speciality, a cup of dry Quaker oats laced with white sugar. Neither Brian nor I could cook and since Gran couldn't stand for more than a few seconds, she wasn't of any help in the kitchen. Even when my cousin Pat later came to live with us as a young teenager, I discovered her cooking abilities were even worse than mine. One time under off-stage directions from my mother, she peeled some potatoes to boil and fried up some slices of Spam but it all went badly wrong. The potatoes boiled dry and burned while the slices of Spam ended up as an unappetising mess stuck to the bottom of the frying pan. I left Pat to it in the kitchen and reverted to my sugared oats. It may not have done my teeth any good but it was better than going hungry.

When I was about eight years old, I decided to join the cubs. There was a thriving cubs and scouts pack based in the church hall just down the street that ran past the back of our house. A couple of my class mates from school who were already members seemed to have fun there so it seemed a good idea to me to join. Overall, I too found my time in the cubs worthwhile and stayed until our final year at Kenilworth Road. I made new friends, enjoyed the activities and games we played as well as learning the different skills required to obtain the various proficiency badges. By the time I left, I had an armful of them up the sleeve of my green uniform sweater. It's perhaps hard to imagine in today's world but I found one of the hardest qualifications to obtain was the telephone badge which was one of the first I did. To pass, I had simply to demonstrate that I could use the telephone by calling Akela, the pack leader one pre-arranged evening at home and having a brief conversation. The Mitchells in the flat downstairs had recently had a public phone installed in the main entrance hall so this was my chance to take the test. I rehearsed what I had to do and what I was going to say many times with my mother in the days leading up to the call. At the appointed time, I went downstairs and stood in trepidation before the wall-mounted device. I quickly ran through one final time the sequence of actions needed and then reached up to lift the receiver, inserted my coin into the slot and dialled Akela's number. When after a few rings she answered, I remembered to push button A on the front of the telephone to complete the connection. I blurted out the couple of sentences I had so carefully memorized and then following a few words of congratulation from Akela, I hung up. I had made my very first telephone call – a small step for mankind maybe but at the time a big step for a small boy.

I always actively took part in the Cubs' annual Bob-a-Job week which mostly took place during the Easter school holidays. I would pair up with another member of our pack and together we would scour the streets of north Leamington, going from door to door to find small jobs to raise money for the Scout movement. The object of this nationwide scheme which had only started in 1949, was for us to do work in the local community in exchange for a shilling or 'bob' as it was commonly called (the equivalent of five pence today). We did all sorts of things such as mowing lawns, cleaning windows, polishing brass lamps or the family's silver cutlery, washing cars and doing the shopping for old ladies. Most people were friendly and helpful but it wasn't easy as all the other cubs and scouts were out on the streets doing the same thing. After the first year of doing Bob-a-Job week, I had an extra reason for joining in each year. I had recognized that there was a need in a few households for someone to do additional work so as we went round, I was always on the lookout for such opportunities. If I felt the householder might have other odd jobs that they wanted doing later, I would offer to come back again in a couple of weeks' time. Each year, I ended Bob-a-Job week with several such possibilities and over the next few weekends I would return, usually with my friend Dennis, to complete the work. Even after splitting the money we received with Dennis, it provided a useful bit of extra income.

It was during my Cub's Bob-a-Job week when I was ten that I first met a family called the Campions who lived in one of the large early Victorian detached villas further north along Kenilworth Road. The first day that I called and rang the door-bell, there was no answer at first and I thought no-one was at home. Then, just as I was about to turn around and try the house next door, a rather scruffy and tired-looking Mrs Campion appeared from around the side of the house. She was dressed in old clothes with dirty wellington boots and holding a garden rake in her hand. When I explained why I had called, a look of relief came over her face and she said I was just the person she needed. She told me she was in the middle of trying to dig out the compost heap in the back garden and was finding it difficult to manage by herself. I was immediately escorted round to the rear of the house by Mrs Campion and quickly put to work for the rest of the morning moving wheel barrows of freshly-dug compost around the garden. At the end of my gardening session, when I went in to the kitchen to wash my hands, Mrs Campion asked me if I would be interested in coming more regularly to help out in the garden. She went on to explain that Mr Campion was partially disabled and could only walk with some difficulty using a pair of crutches and with two young children to look after as well, she was finding it increasingly difficult to stay on top of all the gardening chores. When she added that she would pay me two shillings (10p in today's money) each Saturday for a morning's work, I quickly accepted.

I started my new Saturday job the very next weekend and worked for the Campions most weekends, summer and winter until we moved away from Kenilworth Road. The Campions proved to be an interesting family and as I later learnt from my mother, theirs was an old-established, well-known name in Leamington. They used to own the Campion Hills that bordered on to the brickworks mentioned earlier where we frequently played and beyond which stretched the extensive new council housing estates. These grass-covered hills are the highest area in Leamington, rising to around 300 feet and from the top there is a fine view over the whole town. There were also several streets and buildings in Leamington bearing the Campion name. The family had sold their eponymous hills to the town council during World War II which is presumably where the family's money primarily came from

I liked Mrs Campion right from the start, both she and her husband were friendly, genuine people and very kind to me. I used to arrive on my bike around nine-thirty in the morning and during the summer months my main task was to mow their large back lawn which usually took the best part of two hours using a heavy push mower. At other times, I would trim the hedges, do some weeding or help Mrs Campion dig out the flower beds. The fact that I already knew a little bit about gardening from my earlier Saturday visits to Joan and Andrew in Kenilworth was a help but Mrs Campion always took time to tell me about the plants in the garden and explain the various jobs that needed doing. When it was raining or in the winter, there were always plenty of chores to do inside such as polishing their brass and silver, helping to look after their two young children, Charles and Virginia or even doing a bit of shopping.[7] My working morning always concluded with a cooked lunch with the family, generously provided by the Campions after which I would cycle home to hand over my two shillings to my mother to add to the week's family housekeeping.

A couple of times I also helped Mr Campion with sorting out some of his boxes of files and paperwork in the living room. The first time I did this, I remember seeing a half-full bottle of Johnny Walker red label whisky together with a soda siphon bottle on a side table. I had never seen either of these items before in someone's home and thought they must be very well-off to have such luxuries. Intrigued by the soda syphon, I gave it a little squirt to see

---

[7] Charles Campion would later become famous as a food writer and critic.

what it would do when I was later in the room alone. I also came to know the matriarch of the family, Grandmother Campion, who visited occasionally when I was doing my Saturday morning job. Like her son and daughter-in-law, she was always friendly and encouraging to me. She lived in a first-floor flat in a grand Regency building in Newbold Terrace overlooking the Jephson Gardens at the south end of town. At the end of my first year working for the Campions in 1955, Christmas Eve fell on Saturday and as usual, I went around to their house for the morning. After lunch, Mrs Campion told me that the family was planning to drive over to visit their grandmother later that afternoon for a Christmas tea and much to my surprise, she invited me to join them. I cycled home to check with my mother that this was OK and returned to the Campions' house around 3pm. Soon after, we all piled into their car and drove across town to Newbold Terrace.

Following a rather sumptuous tea, the family started to exchange Christmas gifts and then, much to my surprise, Grandmother Campion handed me a small, white envelope which she smilingly encouraged me to open. Inside I found a crisp, new one-pound note. I think my eyes must have almost popped out of my head as her gift was totally unexpected and it represented a small fortune to a youngster like me. I had never held a ten-shilling note before never mind actually possessing one and was both amazed at her generosity and embarrassed by the fact that I had nothing to give as a present in return. I stammered out my gratitude and apologized for not having a gift but I think the evident pleasure written all over my face was ample recompense for Grandma Campion. It was getting dark by the time we returned to Kenilworth Road and I raced back home on my bike in record time. I couldn't wait to show my mother my wonderful, unexpected Christmas present. She was as stunned as I was at the Campions' kindness. We decided that five shillings would go into the household kitty and with the other half I would open a Post Office savings account in the New Year.

Chapter Nine
RELIGION AND CHOIR

My enduring memories of my mother are those of a quiet, tolerant and charitable person who would always do her best to help others when needed. She never complained about her situation, at least not to me and seemed very conscious that we were better off than many other people, despite our problems. I never heard my mother swear and she hardly ever raised her voice to me or anyone else; she was very calm most of the time. Her reserved nature, which was almost certainly influenced by the stigma relating to her single parent situation, meant that she didn't get involved very much in Leamington's wider society. She did support a couple of charities such as church-run activities that collected money for the lepers and blind in India or Africa. There was always some type of collection box sitting on the mantle shelf in our bedroom into which my mother would put the few coppers that she felt she could spare. She was especially keen on the Anti-vivisection Society and would always stop to sign their petitions when they were campaigning in town. My mother was always fond of animals, particularly cats and we had two of them during our time at Kenilworth Road, first a long-haired Persian called Bobby and then after he died, an ordinary black cat called Sooty. When I was about ten years old, we also acquired a black and white mongrel dog called Blackie (we weren't very imaginative with names for our pets!). Although he was a very even-tempered and likeable dog, he was a bit too lively for Fiona who was always scared of him and sadly, we eventually had him put down by the vet.

My mother was also conservative, both in her outlook and behaviour as well as her political allegiance. She didn't smoke, never used bad language and very rarely drank alcohol other than a glass of sherry or Stone's green ginger wine at Christmas. During our time at Kenilworth Road, the local MP was Sir Anthony Eden who represented the Warwick and Leamington constituency for many years. He had served as Foreign Secretary and was Prime Minister from 1955 to 1957. When he became Prime Minister and his photograph appeared on the front pages of the papers, I remember my mother pointing to his picture and proudly saying she had voted for him and we were so lucky to have him as Prime Minister. From the way she looked at his photograph, I had the feeling that it was perhaps his aristocratic good looks as much as his politics that had garnered my mother's vote for the Conservative Party. In some ways, it was strange that she was a Tory supporter. We were working class, at least as far as our circumstances and situation were concerned, we were relatively poor and received very little from the State but she was never attracted to the wider socialist agenda of the Labour Party or the unions. Had she been alive at the time, I believe my mother would have been a fervent supporter of Margaret Thatcher and her policies of self-reliance, living within one's means and hand-bagging the Communists.

I think she was quite religious and attending church at least once a week was important for her. When we first moved to Leamington, she initially joined the local Baptist Church, just off The Parade in the town centre. She was probably encouraged to join by Mrs Mitchell downstairs as that was the church she went to. Inevitably, I was soon enrolled in their Sunday school which I duly attended almost every Sunday morning and then returned with my mother, Fiona and Mrs Mitchell for the evening service. I remember being impressed by the couple of baptism ceremonies that I witnessed in the church. On the evenings that these took place, there was always an extra-large congregation and the atmosphere inside the church was full of anticipation, almost electric. At the appropriate moment in the service, part of the church floor was removed to reveal a large pool of water into which the people being baptised were briefly but fully submerged by the pastor.

Each Sunday morning as I left for Sunday school, my mother would press a penny or halfpenny coin into my hand which, at the appropriate moment in the service, I carefully placed in one of the church's ubiquitous little wooden collection boxes for their missions somewhere in Africa or India. Over the years, I have occasionally wondered just how much was really achieved through all those regular weekly collections across the country over such a long period. Although there have been some positive results, it seems extraordinary that after a century of giving, we are still being asked to donate to relieve poverty, hunger and disease in these same areas. Greed, corruption, wars and religious rivalry have a lot to answer for. I also question why the churches in Britain concentrated so much effort on charitable activities abroad when there was such desperate post war poverty in our own country.

My mother's involvement with religion and her strong beliefs led to her becoming involved in two rather unusual activities. The first was her membership of the strange and arcane British-Israelites Society whose primary doctrine was based on the belief that the European people and especially those in Britain, were directly descended from the ten lost tribes of Israel. The movement originated in Britain during the heyday of late 19th century British Imperialism and its ideology later spread to parts of the Empire and the USA. I don't know exactly why or when my mother joined the Leamington branch but I do recall Fiona and I being dragged along to periodic evening meetings in a room at the back of a shop at the top of The Parade. Typically, there were twenty or thirty people attending each session which mainly consisted of a lecture and follow-up discussion. These were way above my young head and I found it all extremely boring. The meetings had an aura of quasi-religious fervour and evangelical intensity about them, even though there was no promotion of Judaism *per se*. Sometimes, as we walked home, my mother would try to explain to me the gist of the evening's discussions and a few times I was given small pamphlets to read. One evening when I was about ten, everyone at the meeting was asked to sign some form of membership form or belief pledge, myself included. This didn't make the movement's subsequent meetings any more interesting or intelligible to me but technically, since I have never resigned, perhaps I am still a member of this peculiar organization.

The other unusual religious activity was her long-time involvement with a faith healer called the Reverend Ansty who I think lived in the Birmingham area. He first appeared on the scene when I was nine or ten and it must have been one of my mother's clients that put her in touch with Ansty. Although she never complained about her lot in life, there were inevitably periods when she was low or worried about the future and Ansty was recommended to her as someone who might be able to help. He would arrive in his car, often unannounced, every few months and used to stay for half an hour or so chatting to my mother. His visits always concluded with them both saying some prayers together and finally the laying on of hands – my mother would kneel in front of him and he would place his hands firmly on the top of her head and say a special prayer for her. As he was leaving, my mother would always give him some money but I never saw how much. She always seemed comforted and buoyed up by his visits. I suppose that by having someone with whom she could talk through her problems, these visits were a kind of religious therapy for her. Occasionally, she would tell me about some recent event in which Ansty's faith healing work had brought about a spectacular cure or improvement in the life of one of his widespread flock. There was never the slightest doubt or scepticism in her voice as she related these stories to me and she evidently fully believed in them, no doubt hoping something beneficial would eventually happen for us. I was not so sure or patient, especially after a couple of years of visits without results but maybe it was my fault for nothing enough belief. In some ways, this was just an alternative to the football pools that Pop did – in their different ways they both brought hope to those needed it.

The Reverend's occasional visits continued after we moved to Lillington and lasted at least until I was in my mid-teens. He was about the same age as my mother, tall, dark-haired and friendly while at the same time being quietly authoritative. I can't remember if he was married but he certainly had a son who was a few years older than me and came on one of his visits. In later years, it seemed to me that there was a hard to define intensity and intimacy to Ansty's visits and I think that my mother not only admired and respected the Reverend but also held more than a passing affection for him. If I am right, nothing ever came of it as far as I was aware.

At some stage, Mrs Mitchell became too ill to make the evening walk down to the Baptist Church and my mother's religious allegiance then changed and we started going to the nearby Church of England's Holy Trinity church. This suited my mother since she was C of E anyway and it definitely suited me as not only was the church just a five-minute walk from our house but I also no longer had to go to Sunday school. However, I quickly made up for that by joining the church choir. During the evening service one Sunday, the vicar announced that the church was looking for new members of the choir which in those days was a purely male affair, with a dozen or so boy sopranos plus a similar number of men providing the alto, tenor and bass voices. Normally, at this stage in the service, my mind was drifting off elsewhere; the vicar's announcements about upcoming coffee mornings or meetings of the parochial church council held no interest for me. But somehow this particular announcement about the choir penetrated my reveries and when the vicar said that the choristers received a small quarterly payment, I was hooked.

As we came out of the church after the service, much to my mother's surprise, I told her that I would like to join the choir and immediately went around to the vestry to see the choirmaster, Mr Dexter. When I found him and expressed my interest, he said that I should come to the boys' choir practice next Tuesday evening when he would give me a test to check out my singing abilities. I had never really done any singing before, my voice wasn't particularly strong and I couldn't read music but the possibility of earning some money seemed too good an opportunity to miss. So, a couple of days later, I went back to the church for my voice test. I was called over to stand in front Mr Dexter who sat at a piano with the whole of the boys' choir lined up in the pews behind him. The choirmaster started playing a few scales and asked me to join in following the notes but I was petrified and initially made a real hash of it. However, after a few attempts, I began to get the hang of it. He then tried playing various combinations of notes, asking me to hum either the higher or lower ones which I generally seemed to manage. Finally, he asked me if I could read music and when I said no, I could see that he was not impressed. Not wishing to lose my opportunity, I immediately blurted out that I was willing to learn. The choirmaster turned from the piano to stare at me for a few moments and then with a nod of his head, told me that I could join as a probationary chorister. I was delighted.

One of the other boys took me into the vestry to sort me out with a black cassock, a white surplice plus a frilly white collar and then I was led back to join the rest of the choir. I think I was lucky to have been accepted – it was probably due to a lack of good applicants rather than my singing abilities. Whatever the reason, it turned out to be an important milestone on my life. Not only would I now start to earn some money (we received ten shillings per quarter plus extra for singing at weddings and funerals) but

I would have a new circle of friends and social activities. Also, as I later found out, there was an additional significant cash bonus derived from carol singing around the parish at Christmas time. For a couple of weeks in the run-up to Christmas, we choirboys would tour the streets each evening performing carols outside all the houses. We generally had a good reception from most of the parishioners, often being invited inside for squash, mince pies and chocolates. The money we raised was then split equally between church funds and us boys. The financial aspect of joining the choir was important for me as my mother struggled to give me any regular pocket money. It also meant that I could now help her by making a periodic contribution to the household finances and I usually turned over at least half of whatever I earned to my mother.

The only real problem I experienced during my time in the church choir started a couple of years after I joined. During the morning services, I increasingly began to feel very faint when standing up to sing. The first few times I tried to ignore it and just kept going but then one Sunday, I completely passed out during the *Nunc Dimittis*, collapsing against the shoulder of the boy standing next to me. He was totally unprepared for the arrival of my limp body against his and so he was pushed over into the next boy and so it went down the whole line of choristers until we had all collapsed like ninepins. Pandemonium ensued briefly while the service was stopped and I was dragged out by the curate to the vestry where, a few minutes later after a glass of water, I recovered. A couple of weeks later, much the same thing happened, although this time, my fellow choristers were more alert and there was only a partial choral collapse before I managed to stagger off to the vestry with the help of the curate. I think the news of the church's collapsing choristers soon circulated round the parish as I was certain that church attendance at the morning services rose significantly for a few months. Perhaps unfortunately for the expanded congregation, although my fainting re-occurred intermittently from then on, I was now placed at the end of the row so that I could slip out as soon as I felt faint. Various possible reasons were put forward as to why I was experiencing this problem such as a low intake of liquids and a lack of breakfast (sometimes true but not always). The most likely explanation however, was my approaching puberty combined with the fact that as I later discovered, I have a very low blood pressure.

I soon made good friends with several of the other choristers and in particular, a boy called Robert Sugden. He was the same age as me and lived not far from my former home in Cross Street but in a small crescent of smart detached homes. He went to a private school that was a little further up Kenilworth Road from our house. Suggie as I came to know him had been in the choir for some time and could not only read music but had recently taken the chorister's exam and wore a silver medal around his neck during services to prove it. His parents regularly attended the morning service at our church and always sat in one of the front row pews. Despite our different circumstances, we enjoyed each other's company and usually sat next to each other in the choir stalls as well as regularly spending time together either after choir practice or the church services. His parents were keen church-goers, usually attending the morning service and sitting in the front row of pews. It wasn't long before Suggie introduced me to his parents and after that, I was invited round to his house occasionally for tea. His birthday must have been close to Christmas because I recall going to his birthday party around that time and a few days later his parents took Suggie, his younger sister and me to see a pantomime at the theatre in Coventry. It was the first time I had been to pantomime or even a theatre and I found the whole experience immensely enjoyable.

Although I was impressed by the life-style of the Sugden family and the evident comfort of their home life, I was never jealous. I was simply grateful for the opportunity to occasionally be a part of it and even if our situation in Kenilworth Road fell well short of this level, it was the life we had. We simply got on with it, knowing we were better off than many others. However, contact with families like the Sugdens and Campions showed me what might be possible in the future. Indeed, it was through the time I spent with them that I developed a hope that life could be better together with the ambition to try to make it eventually happen. It also gave me an inkling into what 'normal' family life was like and influenced my thinking and approach to raising my own family when the time came many years later.

Occasionally I was asked by my friends like Suggie if I missed having a dad. It was a simple question from one boy to another but actually one that was very difficult to answer. Whenever this question came up my answer was always the same – no, not really. I explained how I felt that I had more freedom and independence without a father. But in reality, how could I honestly comment on something I had never experienced. I could hardly remember my early life in Canada when my father was around so I didn't really know what having a dad was like. Although my response to the question was true in a limited sense, it was not the whole truth. Of course, I missed having a father around, especially and in my teenage years when trying to acquire many of the life skills that boys usually learn from their fathers such as DIY, sports, learning to drive, career advice etc. I was also old enough to realize that the day to day life of our family would have been much easier if my father had been around to provide for us.

Suggie was with me one day when I voluntarily exposed myself. We were hanging around as usual one spring morning after the Sunday service in the grounds at the back of the church. This large strip of land which was mainly laid out as lawn, lay between the church, the church hall and the scout hut. It provided a play area and social gathering space for the various boys and girls from the choir as well as those from the Cubs, Scouts and Girl

Guides. Depending on the coincidence of activities, there could be anything from half a dozen of us playing around in the gardens to upwards of twenty and ranging in age from nine or ten to the mid-teens. In stark contrast to what might happen today, whenever I was there, I never saw any evidence of any smoking, drugs or alcoholic drinks among any of the various groups. Like most of my school friends, I didn't try my first cigarette (scrounged from my cousin, Brian) until I was fifteen or sixteen and it wasn't an enjoyable experience. Also, there was no peer competition over brand label clothes or the latest mobile phones. Of course, the girls liked to chat about clothes, they always do but we actually talked to each other instead of texting and no-one spent all day inside playing computer games. In this respect, our childhood was both more innocent and less pressurized as well as being less expensive for our parents.

As Suggie and I were standing there chatting all by ourselves, a couple of young teenage girls sauntered over to us. They were Girl Guides, around thirteen or fourteen years old and in their uniforms, having attended a parade prior to the church service. We knew both of them vaguely as they occasionally hung around with the rest of us in the church grounds. After exchanging a few words, the older one, Mary, glanced around to make sure no-one was near and then totally out of the blue asked Suggie and me if one of us would be willing to show her our 'willie'. The pair of us looked at each other in embarrassed surprise as neither of us had ever been propositioned before. Unsure of what to say or do, we both stood there for a few seconds until Mary added she would pay a shilling to the one who agreed. It sounded a good deal to me. I wasn't too worried about Mary seeing my 'willie', after all my mother and sister had seen me in the nude lots of times at home. So, I said OK and Mary led me away like an innocent lamb for the slaughter to an area behind the church hall out of sight of the others. After a short argument about what came first, the reveal or my payment, Mary held out the shilling in one hand and with the other signalled me to begin. I unbuttoned my shorts and then hesitantly pulled them down with my underpants as far as my knees. There really wasn't much for Mary to see since I wasn't yet sexually active and my penis remained un-erect. However, Mary stared at my genitals for a few long seconds while I kept my eyes on the shilling coin in her hand and then before I could move, she reached forward and quickly fondled them. I exclaimed that this wasn't part of the deal but she had already withdrawn her hand. She dropped the shilling on the floor in front of me and ran off giggling to join her friend and the pair of them then disappeared from the churchyard. I pulled up my clothes, picked up my payment and walked out from behind the church hall and back across the lawn to the anxiously waiting Suggie. He asked me if I was OK and while holding tight onto my newly-earned shilling, I replied with a smile that I felt fine and wouldn't mind doing it again.

Unfortunately, at the end of that summer, my friendship with Suggie came to an end. His father was offered a new job in Newcastle-on-Tyne and the family moved up there in late August. As with my earlier friend, Michael in Hong Kong, we promised to write to each other and although we did manage to exchange a couple of letters, life moved on for both of us and the last I heard from him was a card that Christmas. The problem of making good friends and then losing them became an unfortunate, frustrating pattern that was to be repeated several times during my childhood. After Suggie left, going to choir practice or singing at the Sunday services never seemed quite as much fun. However, I did see Mary again occasionally. She was actually a very attractive girl and became popular with some of the scouts, regularly hanging around with them in the garden at the back of the church. She never spoke to me when we saw each other but would usually nod and give me a knowing smile.

There was one other incident involving my genitalia that occurred a few months later at school. Most of my clothes were second-hand, either hand-me-downs given to us by a couple of my mother's clients or purchased at shops such as Joan's pawn shop in town. Generally, this didn't bother me as at that age, I was far from being fashion conscious and many other kids were in the same boat. There was one occasion however, that caused me great embarrassment. Understandably, no-one ever passed on any underwear and so I usually made do with two pairs, one to wear for the week and one in the wash. When I was about ten or eleven years old, my mother was informed by the school that there would be a medical inspection for all the children on Friday morning a couple of weeks later. We both forgot about the upcoming event until the morning of the inspection when, as I started to get dressed, my mother suddenly remembered. Neither of my usual two pairs of underpants were deemed sufficiently presentable and there was no time to wash them, so my mother rummaged around until she found an ancient pair of Brian's in a drawer. They were the old type of woollen pants, stiff and grey-yellow from age and washing. When I tried them on, not only were they too big for me but the button fastening them together at the front was missing. My mother quickly grabbed a large safety pin and stuck the front more or less together saying they would be fine. I wasn't totally convinced but it was getting late so I reluctantly headed off to school.

Later that morning, the boys in our class were called up in groups of six to go for our inspection in the dining hall where we all undressed down to our underpants. Apart from the usual basics of checking our height and weight, listening to our chest and so on, this inspection turned out to be the 'big one' when the doctor leant forward, pulled down the front of our pants and checked our testicles to see if they had dropped. I began to feel uncomfortable in the line-up when the other boys started staring at my odd underpants and safety pin closure but it became worse once I stepped in front of the doctor. As I moved forward to stand before him, the front of my underpants gaped open and my small penis popped out, not exactly the kind of introductory greeting either of us were expecting. Highly embarrassed, I reached down and pushed it back in but when he then tried to lower the front of my pants to get his hands round my testicles, he couldn't as I didn't have the usual elasticated waist band. With the safety pin performing its function of holding my pants tight around my waist, his hand briefly became stuck until I breathed in slightly to allow its release. In the end, I had to undo the safety pin and drop my underpants entirely so that the doctor could carry out his check – all in front of the attendant nurse and the three other boys queuing behind me. I felt embarrassed, humiliated and thoroughly inspected.

I had to endure some ribald comments from a few of my classmates at lunchtime but fortunately, the incident was soon forgotten. When I returned home at the end of the day, I told my mother briefly what had happened and that night, she threw Brian's old pants into the garbage. Better to have no underpants at all than wear those again the next day. However, while I was at school my mother had washed both of my underpants so that normal routine was re-established the following morning. Apart from the suit that my mother bought me for my father's visit and the occasional new shirt or pair of shoes, virtually all my clothes were hand-me-downs or purchased second hand. Other than the incident above with my underpants, this never really bothered me, it was how things were. Fiona was more fortunate in that my mother could make her new dresses and tops from odd bits of left-over material from her work. The first time I can remember going into a shop to buy new clothes was when I was ten or eleven. My mother had been given some special discount coupons for a clothing shop in Coventry so one autumn Saturday afternoon, Brian, Fiona and I all traipsed over there on the bus with my mother. Brian and I both ended up with smart new gabardine raincoats ready for the winter and Fiona came away with a new cardigan and red coat.

The relationship with my sister Fiona during our years at Kenilworth Road was not an easy one. Due to her disabilities, there was only limited interaction between us. Although she couldn't ride a bike or play ball games, we did spend some time together at weekends or during my school holidays. She liked to play simple card games with me such as *Snap* and *Happy Families*, doing children's small jigsaws or colouring in pictures in her drawing books. Together with my mother, I tried to teach her to write but all she could really manage were the initials of her name 'FH' – strangely, she always wrote the 'F' backwards. We were quite unable to persuade her to write it the proper way around. She loved to creep up and try to tickle one of us and then be chased and tickled herself. When she was caught, she would let out a piercing squawking scream and then burst into giggles – it was her favourite game. Like most Down's syndrome children, my sister was a gentle soul; quiet, unassuming and affectionate she engendered in turn, much love from those who knew her. She was rarely moody, never cried (unless physically hurt) or caused us any problems, apart from her occasional escapes from the flat. Of course, there were times when I felt it would be good to have a 'normal' sister, especially when I was older – someone to confide in or share problems with. And although I knew she was at the heart of our situation, I never blamed her for that. It was an issue that lay firmly at the door of our parents.

Chapter Ten
COUSINS BRIAN AND PAT

Some months after I last heard from Suggie, I gradually got to know a small group of boys at my junior school in Lillington, Andrew, Richard, Clive and Barry and we eventually became the best of friends. We were a disparate quintet with quite different backgrounds. Andrew lived just a couple of hundred yards round the corner from my house where his parents owned a small hotel called Arden House which was next door to the Leamington College for Boys, the local grammar school. He was the one I came to know first and we regularly played together in their garden at the back of the hotel. If his father and younger brother were around we often played French cricket together or if it was raining, a game of Monopoly inside. Sometimes I was invited to stay for lunch which was served in the hotel restaurant after all the guests had finished. It felt odd to be seated at a dining table with Andrew and I being served lunch by a waitress but it was all quite normal for my friend. Richard's home was in a small village a couple of miles outside Leamington where his parents ran a small-holding. Clive, who was the most serious of our gang, came from a relatively well-off family that lived in a large flat on the top floor of a substantial late-Victorian red brick building in Arlington Avenue, not far from me. His house had extensive, creepy cellars with heavy steel doors that Clive told us had been used as a bomb shelter during the War.

Barry lived in Covent Garden Market, an area of small late-Georgian terraced homes at the back of The Parade. The original market had ceased functioning soon after the War and the homes here were now mostly in such bad condition that the area was regarded as a slum and eventually demolished some ten years later. Barry was the entertainer in our group in that he was very good at impressions and telling jokes. When he was round at my house, he would often have my mother and me in stitches with his amusing antics. If Barry was the funny guy, I was the tough guy or enforcer. I wasn't the tallest or strongest boy at school but in my last year or two there, I was definitely the toughest and no-one dared to pick a quarrel with me. If there were arguments or fights in the playground, it was usually me the other boys turned to in order to sort things out. Although I was mostly a happy-go-lucky type of child, I had a hard edginess to my character that I think must have derived from learning to stand up for myself when I used to play a lot with Brian and his friends who were much older than me.

Despite our differing backgrounds and personalities, the five of us became close friends and we spent a lot of time together, especially during the holidays. Although our adventures were not as romantic or idyllic as those described in Enid Blyton's books about the Famous Five, we still had great fun. Since we all had bikes, we would arrange to rendezvous somewhere and then cycle off for the rest of the day to explore the lanes and countryside around Leamington. I can remember playing in woods filled with bluebells in the spring, spending the whole afternoon building a series of dams in a stream and racing our bikes down a steep hill near Richard's house. Our favourite haunt was a rather dilapidated old mill in a hamlet on the River Avon just a couple of miles north of Leamington. At the time, this large building was used as a warehouse or store, possibly by a local antiques dealer as it was crammed full of an amazing variety of furniture and bric-a-brac. Although the mill was always locked up when we visited, it wasn't secure enough to keep out our little gang and we soon found a way in through a window. Once inside, the building and its apparently abandoned contents provided us with endless hours of entertainment. We re-arranged some of the furniture on the first floor one day to make ourselves a den where we sat and looked at some of the many books stacked in cardboard boxes. There were various bits of old sporting equipment lying around such as golf clubs and cricket bats which provided the basis for all sorts of games. During one visit, we discovered several boxes of what were probably billiard balls and we took these up to the top floor and then had great fun dropping them down through the open centre of the building and into the water running through the bottom of the mill. As I write about this now, I realize it was a senseless and stupid thing to do but such thoughts were far from the minds of ten-year-old boys like us.

The independence and freedom we enjoyed then is perhaps hard to understand now in an age when most parents exert a much tighter control and supervision over their children's lives. Of course, there was much less traffic on the roads in those days and the whole area was less urbanized or developed. However, that didn't mean that some of the risks and dangers faced by children today were also not present then, as evidenced by the earlier story about the man who exposed himself to me in the street. Although statistical sources vary, the numbers of child murders and abductions today is similar to those in the 1950s, perhaps even slightly lower when adjusted for the rise in population, as are deaths and serious injuries from road accidents. But the attitude then of society in general and as far as I am aware of our parents in particular, seems to have been much more relaxed about what we did and where we went. Apart perhaps from Clive's mother who was a little bit prissy at times, it was rare for any of our parents to ask us where we were going when we went out to play. I might be reminded to be back in time for tea or to return later to deliver a completed dress to a client but that was about it. However, I did get a very occasional thrashing from my mother when she caught me misbehaving, something that probably wouldn't happen today but as I usually deserved it, I accepted it and it never did me any long-term harm, physically or mentally. The only real parallel with today was the legal requirement not to leave young children at home alone. In a way, it was odd that I couldn't be left alone at home but was free to wander the streets by myself at all hours.

For most of the time that Brian lived with us, our relationship was fine and normal but we were never close, partly because of our age difference and different temperaments. My mother treated us both equally and we did a lot of things together in the early years such as our joint holidays in London and Weston Super Mare. We were both at the same school initially and when I joined the local cubs, Brian soon became a scout with the same troop. Some months after Brian arrived, we were both enrolled by my mother for private piano lessons with a lady in Warwick Place. It was a strange decision because neither of us had exhibited any interest in learning to play an instrument and as we didn't have a piano at home, there was no way for us to practice. We shared a one-hour session between us but the lessons didn't last very long. Neither of us showed any real aptitude and without a piano to practice on, we weren't making much progress. I think our teacher must have said as much to my mother because after a couple of months, she suddenly announced that we didn't have to go to these lessons any more. We were both glad that her attempt to imbue the pair of us with a small amount of culture had ceased and I think she was too, since we couldn't really afford it. In later life, I have always greatly envied those who could play a musical instrument well and regretted that I didn't show more aptitude or persistence when I had the chance.

We argued occasionally as any two boys might but it never led to any serious fighting. Although Brian was five years older than me, so taller and stronger, he never really abused his physical advantage with me. When I wasn't out playing with my friends, we would often spend time together, sitting chatting in his bedroom or reading comics. I regularly joined him when he went out to play with his friends and was always included in their games. One of their favourite pass-times on summer evenings was to go to the fields around the brickworks that existed then close to the Campion Hills, about half a mile from our house. There was a steep cliff at one end that marked the edge of old clay extraction workings and the boys would dare each other to try to walk along the face of the cliff from one end to the other without falling down. It was not too difficult when it was dry but if there had been any rain, it was hard to get a purchase on the slippery clay soil. If you dithered, the rest of the group encouraged you to move forwards by pelting you from below with small balls of clay. Interest in this game eventually waned when all of us had successfully made the crossing several times and it was replaced by something much more exciting and dangerous.

It took a while for the new game to fully develop but basically, we split up into two teams and went across to the clay pits alongside the brickworks. Each team crouched down behind the mounds of clay opposite each other and we would then start throwing balls of clay at the other side until one team gave up and evacuated their position. With half a dozen boys on each team, the stream of clay balls being thrown was considerable plus the older boys like Brian, were able to heave much larger lumps across the divide than a ten-year-old like me. The game might go on for twenty or thirty minutes and regardless of which team you were on, it was impossible to avoid being hit at least once. If you were struck by one of the bigger balls thrown by the older boys, it hurt a lot and several times I had bruises on my arms and legs when I got home.

Another of the favourite play areas for Brian and his friends in the summer was the park located at the top of the Parade which provided a playground haven for young teenagers. I often tagged along and joined in their games which usually consisted of chasing and fighting other groups of boys in the thickets of trees and bushes around the park. After an hour or two, we were usually dirty and sweaty, often with rips in our clothing and as we trailed home, we must have looked like extras from the cast of the

Lord of the Flies film. We may have had on more clothing than the boys in the film but our games were often just as ferocious and violent. Activities with older boys like these were all frantically exciting for a younger boy like me and through such play I developed a certain toughness and bravado that was to prove useful in the future.

Life with Brian did not always run smoothly however and there were a couple of incidents that later caused a rift to develop between us. The first occurred one summer during a cubs and scouts weekend camping trip that we both went on. The camp was held in a muddy farmer's field just outside a village to the south of Leamington with packs from all over the local area. As far as I remember it, the weather was dreadful; it poured the afternoon of our arrival while we set up the camp and continued to rain most of the weekend. Out tents proved inadequate to deal with the constant downpours and our bedding soon got damp. Due to the weather, the much-anticipated outdoor evening cook-outs and song-singing around the camp fire also mostly proved a wash-out. However, the worst part of the weekend came on the last day when Brian threw my dinner plate and cutlery into the middle of the large cesspit that had been dug on the edge of the camp site. I can't remember now exactly why he did this - I think we had some kind of argument – but it was just before lunch was to be served. I was hungry and now without a plate I couldn't eat. I had no choice but to take off my shoes and socks and wade into the pit to try to retrieve my things. The plate was reasonably easy to get as it was sticking up out of the pile of excrement but finding my knife and fork proved more difficult and required a certain amount of prodding around with my feet until I could find them and raise them up sufficiently to grab them. By the time I had washed off the disgusting mess from my hands, legs and plate, lunch was almost over and all I could find were some lukewarm baked beans. I don't think I fully erased the stench from my body until I got home and had a hot bath.

In Brian's mind, this was probably just a boyish prank, an unpleasant one certainly for me but not the end of the world. However, much more serious was another event that occurred about a year later at home. One day, Brian came home with an air pistol that he had borrowed from one of his friends and started playing with it in the house. Naturally, he showed it to me and I followed him into his bedroom where he began firing a few shots from his window into the empty garden below. This was all quite harmless and seemed good fun but all of a sudden, he turned round and said he was going to shoot me. In terror, I darted out of his bedroom and down the back hallway with Brian close behind, waving the air pistol around. Then, just as I was heading up the stairs towards our living room, I felt a sting in my leg just above the ankle. Brian had shot me, I couldn't believe it and cried out, more in shock than real pain. At the sound of my cry, my mother appeared and was confronted by the sight of me in tears lying across the stairs with Brian standing over me holding the pistol. She shouted at Brian to drop the pistol and to go to his room immediately which he did. My mother tried to get the pellet out but it had gone too deep so the doctor had to be sent for to sort me out. My mother was so terrified at what had happened that she also called the police with the upshot that a few days later, Brian was sent away to a juvenile home near Birmingham. I was never completely sure that Brian really meant to shoot me, he may have just pulled the trigger in the heat of chasing after me. But then he was fourteen at the time and should have been aware of how stupid and potentially dangerous his actions were.

After almost a year away, my mother finally allowed Brian to come back and live with us again but perhaps understandably, his relationship with both my mother and I was changed. He was now fifteen, almost a man and would soon leave school to start work which he duly did a few months later, taking up an apprenticeship at a car repair garage in Kenilworth. However, this job only lasted less than twelve months; Brian found it too boring and disliked the daily bus journey between Leamington and Kenilworth. For a while, he worked as an assistant projectionist in a local cinema until one evening in the summer of 1956, he came home and announced that he had joined the Royal Navy, together with his best friend Phil. Shortly afterwards he left home to start his training in the Navy and we didn't see him again for almost another two years.

The only other significant event involving Brian and me was an incident for which I was almost entirely responsible. On his sixteenth birthday, my mother bought Brian a new watch, nothing fancy but it had the useful feature of a large hand to mark the seconds. A week or two later, it so happened that at school we were preparing for our annual sports day. I was involved in several of the boys' field events and our teacher had suggested that some of us should go and practice on the running track marked out on the school sports field. Most of the boys had watches and so were able to time themselves doing laps around the track. Since I didn't have a watch, I couldn't time myself and so was unsure of how my lap times compared with the other boys. But I knew where I could get a watch.

Brian didn't normally wear his watch during the day to his job at the garage as it might get damaged and so a couple of days later when the next sports practice session was due, I went to Brian's room to borrow his watch for the day. I carefully put it in my pocket and went off to school and that afternoon, I was able to time myself doing the hundred yards. When we compared times, I was as pleased as punch to find I was the second fastest. After the practice, we returned to our classroom where I put Brian's watch safely away in my desk. At the end of the day, I rushed out of class and headed home as normal, completely forgetting about the watch. It wasn't till tea-time when Brain mentioned that he couldn't find his watch that I realized my error. When my mother said that it would surely turn up somewhere and Brian should have a more careful search round the house for it, I decided to slip out and cycle back to school to retrieve the watch from my desk. Of course, when I got there, I found that the school was all securely locked up and there was no way to collect Brian's watch. When I returned home an hour or so later, it seemed as if all hell had broken loose in the house. While I had been away, Brian and my mother had diligently searched our flat but naturally found nothing and so my mother had called the police. This was a strange and unexpected thing for her to do as the watch was not especially valuable and it was unclear exactly what the police could do. Anyway, when I walked in, there were two detectives standing in our living room talking to my mother and Brian. They had not only responded remarkably quickly but as I later learnt, they had turned our flat upside down, interviewed the Husseys, searched the Mitchell's garden and even been through the dustbins.

Now their attention was fully focussed on me and one of the detectives asked me if I knew anything about the missing watch. At first I tried to prevaricate but I am not a good dissembler and probably looked guilty from the moment I walked in. The pair of detectives soon had the full story out of me and they then told my mother that they would take me back to school to check out my story and if true, retrieve the watch. I was escorted out to their car which was parked outside our house, locked into the back and driven to my school. During the journey, the detectives frequently turned around and threw accusations at me – '*I was lying, I'd really sold the watch and it wasn't at school, I was an extremely naughty boy*' and '*did I realize how serious this was?*' I was totally distraught and under this barrage of questions I became very anxious and frightened. I needed to go to the lavatory and pleaded with the detectives to let me out of the car. Either they didn't believe me or thought that if they let me out I would somehow run off and escape so they refused saying I must wait until we reached the school. As they drove on, I knew I couldn't hold it anymore and suddenly to my complete horror, a stream of urine poured into my shorts and all over the back seat. It didn't take long for the detectives to smell my urine and they now tore into me with a stream of invective – I was now '*a dirty, pissing, little thief*' and '*did I regularly piss in my pants?*'

By the time we reached the school, I was shaking with terror. The detectives soon found the caretaker who opened up the front door and we all marched to my classroom where the missing watch was retrieved from my desk. Once we returned home and handed the watch back to Brian, I thought that would be the end of the matter but the detectives had other ideas. They told my mother that I would now have to accompany them to the police station where the full details of the incident would be recorded and a report filed. My mother protested but the detectives insisted and still in my sodden shorts, I was driven to the police station. By now I was almost completely comatose and only vaguely remember the events in the police station. I was handed over to the desk sergeant and taken to an interview room where I was questioned at length, reminded about how serious this matter was and finally told that the report on my criminal activity would be held on file by the police in case I did it again. Eventually, I was driven home again and dumped outside our house. Inside, everyone was upset, most of all me. A moment of stupidity and simple forgetfulness by me had led to a sequence of events that spiralled out of control, resulting in great humiliation for me and embarrassment for my mother. None of us ever spoke about the incident again.

Like my Gran and Brian before her, my cousin Pat arrived to live with us one Sunday afternoon, courtesy once more of Uncle Joe and Auntie Mary. I was almost eleven at the time and Pat was three years older than me. I had met her a year or so earlier when she had come over for a week to visit her brother Brian. I'm not entirely sure why my mother had agreed to now take on this extra burden. From the little she told me, I gathered Joe and Mary claimed that Pat had expressed the wish to live with her brother instead of being separated but the real reason was that they were finding Pat a bit of a handful. She was a lively, precocious young teenager with dark, shoulder-length, wavy hair and was developing fast physically, if not mentally. I think my mother's decision may have been influenced by the fact that by looking after Pat, she would receive a regular monthly payment from Social Services as she had been doing for Brian. Although there would obviously be a cost of feeding and clothing Pat, my mother must have felt that the benefit of a regular income outweighed the potential disadvantages. Pat duly moved into the vacant back bedroom and I now had to adjust to having a female teenager around the house.

Whatever Pat's problems had been at Joe and Mary's, she seemed to settle down fairly quickly with us. Although she and Brian didn't seem to be particularly close, the presence of her brother was probably a contributory factor to her improved behaviour while we were at Kenilworth Road. However, Pat's sexual precociousness later became an increasing problem and during her stay with us she had a string of older boyfriends chasing after her which my mother did her best to fight off. It became more acute in 1956 when Pat took a Saturday job at a ladies' clothes shop and therefore had a bit of money to spend on going out. Strict rules were laid down by my mother concerning where Pat could go and what time she had to be home by and to be fair to her, these were mostly adhered to. The only other problem relating to Pat was due to her name when she initially started at Milverton School. My cousins' surname was Green, never an issue for Brian but at school, P Green was an unfortunate juxtaposition that her parents should have foreseen. The combination of being a new girl with an odd name meant that Pat became the butt of teasing by her female classmates which simply reinforced her interest in boys.

I soon learned that Pat wasn't interested in any of my games or hobbies - she spent most of her free time reading girls' magazines or talking to boys at the front door – so there was little interaction between us. However, we did share an odd experience one night at home. Because we had no front door as such to our flat, my mother always locked her bedroom door when she went to bed. Hers was the only room in the house apart from the bathroom to have a lockable door. If she had a particularly busy day this could be as early as eight or nine in the evening. In summer, I often stayed out playing until it was almost dark and sometimes on such occasions when I came home, I would find the bedroom door locked. If I could see light coming from under the door, I knew my mother was reading in bed so I would gently knock and she would let me in. But very occasionally, when everything was dark, I knew my mother was sleeping and so I would quietly wander down the corridor to try to persuade Brian to let me into his room and sleep with him in his bed.

One such Saturday night however, Brian had a couple of friends round and didn't want to let me in so I tried Pat's room next door at the end of the corridor. I could see her light was still on and so I knocked gently on the door and explained my predicament. I half expected her to refuse me but she opened the door and seemed quite happy to let me in. She had evidently been reading in bed and once I was in the room, she quickly hopped back under the covers and went back to looking at her girl's magazine. Without looking at me, she patted the right side of her bed to indicate where I could sleep and I quickly undressed down to my underpants. I hopped into the bed and lay down beside her. After half an hour or so, Pat stopped reading and turned off the light, leaving us both to settle down to sleep.

I was just reaching the point of totally drifting off when in my semi-conscious state, I thought I heard a noise at the door. As I half-raised my head off the pillow I clearly heard the door handle gently rattling in the catch. Pat had obviously heard it too and was now sitting bolt-upright alongside me in the bed. We were both petrified and remained totally immobile as some unseen hand grasped the doorknob once more, turning it gently back and forth a few times. I could hear heavy breathing on the other side of the door and when a drunken man's voice asked if there was anyone inside, I was so terrified, despite my normal bravado, that I momentarily lost control of my bladder and partially wet Pat's bed. After jiggling the door handle a couple more times, I then heard the man's shuffling footsteps retreating down the corridor and then slowly making their way up the creaking staircase to the flat above.

Once all was quiet again, Pat half-whispered to me that it was Mr Hussey, our Irish neighbour from upstairs. She explained that this performance had happened several times before on a Saturday night and although he had never actually opened the door, Pat was almost as scared as I was that he would come into her bedroom. Knowing it was Saturday, that was why she had been happy to let me into her room, thinking I might be some form of protection that night if Mr Hussey showed up. I was embarrassed at not only having failed in my protective duties but also having wet my side of the bed. However, Pat didn't seem to mind too much and as she stripped the sheets from the bed, she said that it was good to have had someone else with her. I went off to the bathroom to clean myself up and rinse through my soiled underpants. By the time I returned with a towel wrapped around my middle, Pat was back in bed so I switched off the light and hopped back in bed. We were both soon fast asleep. The next morning when I saw my mother, I explained what had happened and she immediately rushed upstairs to confront Mr Hussey. I don't know what was said but it was the last time that Pat was disturbed by the Irish door knob rattler.

Chapter Eleven
A TRAGIC END

Although I enjoyed participating in the usual school sporting activities as well as our various games at cubs, there were few opportunities to take part in any other organized sports. There simply didn't seem to be the wide range of activities for youngsters that are almost taken for granted today. Running around outside while playing with my friends or riding my bike to and from school were my main physical activities. My only regular organized exercise was swimming during the periodic school visits to the Leamington baths. Each class at our junior school had an allocated swimming morning or afternoon once a month when the whole class was transported in a hired coach to the public baths behind the Royal Pump Rooms at the lower end of town. This was not something I looked forward to as I have never been particularly good at swimming and didn't enjoy it. I suppose that my dislike of swimming originated with my father throwing me into the pool one day in Canada when I was about three years old. It was a sink or swim moment and as I couldn't swim I sunk to the bottom of the pool. My father, who was an excellent swimmer, dived in and pulled me out but not before I had ingested a lot of water and developed an instant fear of the water and drowning.

As a non-swimmer, initially on these school trips to the baths, I joined the group taking beginner's lessons at the shallow end of the pool. After a couple of these sessions, I began to get the hang of the breast-stroke and could swim a few yards without the aid of any flotation devices. At the end of each of our lessons, there was a general swim-time during which we were allowed to play around in the pool as we wanted. Over-impressed with my new swimming ability, I walked along the pool edge to join a couple of my more able friends who were playing around in the deep end. I couldn't dive yet so I backed up a few steps and then took a running leap into the middle of the pool. I sank down into the depths of the water for what seemed like ages until I touched the bottom and then, pushing off, slowly rose back up to the surface. Choking and spluttering out water, I tried to get into a more horizontal position to start doing my breast-stroke but nothing seemed to work. I found myself sinking down once more to the bottom and in my breathless state I swallowed a lot more water. When I finally resurfaced, I was in a complete panic, gasping for air and thrashing around helplessly. As I began to go under for the third time, I felt someone grab my arms and I was hauled to the side of the pool which I then clung onto literally for dear life. Fortunately, my friends had realized my predicament and had come to my rescue. They bobbed up and down in the water grinning at me until I eventually got my breath back and slowly hauled myself out of the pool. Still coughing up water, I ignominiously returned to the shallow end of the pool.

After this experience, I conveniently forgot to take my swimming trunks and towel to school for the rest of that term's visits to the pool. My teacher's annoyance at my 'forgetfulness' was worth enduring to avoid going back into the pool. However, the excuse of having forgotten my swimming things couldn't work forever and the following term I was once more obliged to join the monthly trips to the baths. Although I did eventually learn to swim and dive, I was never a very confident swimmer and have always retained a deep-down fear of water, whether in swimming pools or the sea.

As far as I can remember, I was the only child in either of my schools from a one parent family, at least until my final year in junior school when a new boy called Malcolm arrived who also lived with his divorced mother. This parental uniqueness never seemed strange or odd to me at the time. No-one at school ever spoke to me about it, made comments or asked questions and I never experienced any awkward moments in this regard. Of course, there were a few brief moments when I regretted the lack of a father but mostly, there seemed little point in thinking about it. Nothing was going to change and along with the rest of my family, I simply got on with whatever life served up. Malcolm and I became good friends for a while even though he was in a different class. His home was not far from mine and after school, we would often ride home together. We were drawn to each other because of our shared family situation, both of us finding it interesting to be able to chat to another boy in a similar position and share experiences.

It was from Malcolm that I first came across the term *mental breakdown.* As we were sitting on our bikes one afternoon outside a local sweet shop, he told me that his mum was seeing the doctor a lot as she was having a mental breakdown. His gran had just arrived to stay and look after him. I'm not sure how much young Malcolm understood about his mother's problem but although I could tell from his tone that it was something serious, I had no idea what mental illness meant. When I got home later that day, I rushed up to my mother and said 'mummy, what's a mental breakdown'. She was understandably shocked by both the abruptness of my query and that I should ask such a strange question out of the blue. I explained my reason for asking but my mother was reticent to talk much about it and so I wasn't much wiser on the subject after our brief chat. Attitudes towards mental breakdowns in the mid-fifties were quite different from today; most people didn't like to talk about it and if they did, it was in a hushed tone of voice. It was odd that my mother reacted this way. She was relatively broad-minded and open about most things and we had our own form of mental illness in the family with my sister.

After a couple of months, my friendship with Malcolm waned and we saw much less of each other. Apart from our single parent backgrounds, we had little in common with no shared interests or friends. Our initial curiosity about each other's life had been sated and we largely went our separate ways. Shortly before the end of term that summer, Malcolm told me that his mother had been taken away to a special hospital and that he was leaving Leamington in a few days to go to live with his grandparents. He was clearly upset and I felt very sorry for him but couldn't really think of anything suitable to say. I knew I would be desperately unhappy if my mother had been taken away and I was left to be looked after by my great grandmother. As he walked away, I shouted after him 'I hope your new school's alright' – it was the only thing that came into my mind. We never saw each other again

One of my mother's strangest but nonetheless interesting acquaintance was an old Jewish lady called Gretcha who lived in a bedsit on the top floor of a building in Clarendon Square. Today, the tall, fine Victorian stuccoed buildings surrounding this square are highly desirable residences but in the early 1950s they were mostly run-down tenement flats occupied by some of the poorest families in Leamington. Gretcha's garret was tiny, it was up four flights of stairs and while it had gas there was no electricity supply so her couple of rooms were lit solely by wall-mounted gas lamps. Its only redeeming feature was the large window that looked out across the square. As far as I recall, Gretcha was originally from somewhere in eastern Europe, possibly Austria or Hungary and had arrived in Britain at the start of the War. She had a slight hunchback and suffered from arthritis which over the years that I came to know her, increasingly limited her movements so that eventually, she hardly left her small flat. Despite her disabilities, she was a lively and fascinating old woman, much interested in classical music (her wind-up gramophone was almost always on when I went around), reading and especially doing large jigsaw puzzles. I don't know how Gretcha and my mother met but they had shared interests in music and reading and somehow my mother seemed to have taken Gretcha under her wing. Sometimes at weekends, my mother wold ask me to pop round to Gretcha's flat with some food, maybe a few slices from our roast joint or a couple of eggs and some bread – she otherwise seemed to exist on little more than tea and toast. At other times, my mother, Fiona and I would visit Gretcha for an afternoon cup of tea. Whenever we went, Gretcha was always in the middle of one of her giant 1000-piece jigsaws, laid out on a table in front of the window. She would usually ask me in her heavily-accented English to help fill some of the gaps in the puzzle as my eyesight and nimble fingers were better than hers.

Over time, I suppose she became a kind of surrogate grandmother and if my mother had to go out to the shops or see a client, I would walk round to Gretcha's with Fiona for an hour or so. Gretcha also encouraged me to call in on my way back from school occasionally for a cup of tea and a biscuit. I think she enjoyed having someone to talk to, even a youngster like me and my growing ability with jigsaws was always welcomed. One such afternoon, as I was leaving her building, I met one of my school friends outside who lived around the corner. He was surprized to see me there and asked me what I was doing. As we talked, I started swinging around on the black iron railings that ran across the front of the flats but then I suddenly lost my footing and slipped forward, banging the top of my head into a thick overhanging spike on the railings. Suddenly there was blood everywhere and the pain in my skull was excruciating. I asked my friend to look at the wound and see how bad it was but he went very pale and all he seemed able to say was that it was bleeding a lot. I reached into my pocket and pulled out my handkerchief which I then tried to hold on top of my head to staunch the bleeding. I wasn't sure what to do next. I could try to stagger back up the stairs to Gretcha's flat but I wasn't sure she could help and in that time, I could almost be home. So, I left my friend standing there gawping at me and set out for home.

As I staggered along, one hand on top of my head holding my bloodied handkerchief and trickles of blood running down my face, I must have presented an odd sight. I passed a couple of people in the street but no-one asked if I was alright or needed help. After a few minutes, I made it back home and found my mother who was shocked to see the state I was in. I was quickly ushered into the bathroom where she washed off the wound and having inspected it, immediately called the doctor. As it turned out, the damage as not too serious. I had a slight dent in my skull but nothing broken and with a few stitches and a bandage patched onto the top of my head, I was sent to bed early to rest and pronounced fit for duty. Fortunately, there were no after-effects although on subsequent visits to Gretcha's over the next few weeks, the dark stains of my blood were still visible around the steps of her house.

Early one Saturday spring evening when I was eleven years old, my mother was looking down into the street from our living room window when she exclaimed 'That's very odd'. I rushed over to see what she was looking at and immediately saw what she was referring to. Isobel, our life-long spinster neighbour from downstairs was walking down Kenilworth Road, heading towards town with a man on her arm. Neither of us could believe our eyes. In all the time we had lived in this flat, we had never, ever seen Isobel with anyone other than her mother. But over the next few months, Isobel and her new man became a regular sight. However, when my mother spoke to Mrs Mitchell about the developing relationship a few days after our first sighting of the couple, it was clear that Isobel's mother was not at all happy with this unexpected turn of events. Apparently, they had met in a local pub where Isobel, who liked a drink or two, had been a regular for some time. Mrs Mitchell's concern was not that she objected to Isobel finding a man, rather it was the type of man she had found. He was short, rough-mannered, uneducated and worked as a barman in the pub where he and Isobel first met. As we later discovered, he also swore a lot, drank heavily and then became violent.

A week or two after first seeing Isobel and her man walking down Kenilworth Road, Dennis and I happened to be playing in the street when we noticed the couple pass by, once again heading for town. Our favourite game at the time was to sneak up and down the backstreets pretending we were spies. On seeing Isobel and her boyfriend, we instantly decided it would be fun to hone our spying skills by following them and investigating this unexpected relationship further. We let them walk ahead for twenty or thirty yards and then started after them, sidling along the pavement, dodging into doorways or crouching behind convenient walls and trees. Giggling and whispering to each other, we pursued our quarry to the end of Kenilworth Road, down the top part of The Parade and then on into Covent Garden Market where they disappeared into a pub. We waited outside the pub for a while but it was obvious they would be in there for some time so we ambled back home. As far as we could tell, they had been oblivious to our pursuit and we therefore felt very proud of our improving spy skills.

Over the next six months, as Isobel's relationship with her new boyfriend became stronger, we saw them together much more frequently and she started bringing him home, much to Mrs Mitchell's annoyance and disgust. Dennis and I played our new game of following them into town a couple more times but we soon tired of being spies. Then early one morning there was an urgent knocking at our bedroom door and when my mother opened it, Isobel came in and announced to my mother that Mrs Mitchell had died in the night. Although we knew that she had been suffering from a heavy cold for a few days, this news came as a shock. My mother went downstairs with Isobel to call the doctor and to start to sort things out. I had never seen a dead body and out of curiosity, I started to follow my mother but was quickly and firmly told to go back to the bedroom and stay there with Fiona. Mrs Mitchell was buried a week later after a small funeral service at the Baptist Church which my mother attended. Soon after the funeral, it became evident that Isobel's boyfriend had moved in with her and our original impression of him did not improve with closer acquaintance. He was ugly, foul-mouthed, often drunk in the house and violent; Isobel must have been truly desperate to have stuck with this man. As time went by, we increasingly heard the pair of them arguing loudly in their flat and he must have been hitting Isobel as we occasionally saw her with bruises on her face. Later that year we left Kenilworth Road to move to a new house but soon after, my mother learnt that Isobel's man had left her and a few days later, she had committed suicide in her flat by slitting her wrists. It was a tragic end to what had been a rather sad and lonely life.

Chapter Twelve
LEAVING FOR LILLINGTON

At some stage early in the summer term of 1956, I started going out with Janet Nicholson who was in the same class as me at Lillington school and sat just a couple of desks away. She was slim, about the same height as me and had short, light-brown hair with a few tiny freckles scattered across her face. For several weeks, she and another girl called Jennifer had somehow attached themselves to my small group of friends during our break times in school. I didn't object because I actually quite liked her. She was lively, fun to talk to and she joined in our games without being at all tomboyish. I think our relationship started when Dennis and I plus the two girls met up after school one day to play in the sports fields off Lillington Road, behind Leamington College. We were having great fun careering around on our bikes and chasing after each other until two young teenage boys arrived on the scene. Much to our annoyance, they started to jump in front of us, trying to make us fall off our bikes, especially Janet and Jennifer. Dennis and I rode up to the two boys and asked them to stop and leave us alone but they said if we didn't like it, we should leave. Although both boys were bigger than me, I felt I had to do something in front of the girls so I clenched my fist and hit one of them squarely in the face, knocking him to the ground. The other boy started to move forward but then hesitated and with Dennis aggressively backing me up, the pair of them decided they were the ones who would leave. My hand and wrist now ached from the blow but when Janet took my wounded hand in hers and gave me an admiring glance, I felt that it was worth the pain. It was at that moment I decided to invite Janet out on a date.

At that time, several of us boys would occasionally go to the cinema on a Saturday morning and on the Friday before our next visit, I plucked up enough courage to ask Janet to come as well. At first, I thought she was going to turn me down as she paused a while before replying. But then she broke into a smile and asked me who was paying. Inexperienced as I then was in the intricacies of dating girls, this was not an answer I had anticipated. It was hard enough for me to save up enough money for one ticket never mind two but the thought of sitting in the back row of the cinema with Janet was enough to cause me to instantly blurt out that I would pay. However, although I didn't think of it until later, I had a secret that Janet didn't know about. At the time, my cousin Brian was working as an assistant projectionist each weekend at the cinema and I knew he sometimes got free tickets. So that evening, I explained my little problem to Brian and he agreed to get me a free ticket for the Saturday morning show which he would leave at the ticket office.

The following morning, I cycled down to the cinema which was at the far end of town near the Victoria Park. I had learned enough about dates from Brian and Pat to know that I should be there first and I arrived ridiculously early, almost half an hour before the appointed time. I sat on my bike near the cinema entrance nervously watching and waiting to see if Janet would turn up. The minutes dragged by and as an ever-increasing number of boys and girls arrived and went in to the cinema, many of them schoolmates. Then, just as I was beginning to think she wasn't coming, I saw her familiar head bobbing up and down as she furiously pedalled her bike down the street towards me and the cinema. We quickly added our bikes to the stack of dozens of others round the back of the cinema building and rushed in. While Janet went to buy some sweets, I went to the ticket office to purchase my ticket while surreptitiously collecting the free ticket which Brian had left in an envelope for me. When we went into the cinema, I was disappointed to find in the semi-darkness that the back row of the stalls was already full. The only pair of seats together were much further forwards near the screen so I reluctantly steered Janet over towards them and we sat down. The lights soon went down and the morning's programme started. I have absolutely no recollection of what film we watched - it was probably a Western - as my interest lay elsewhere. Janet and I sat holding hands through the whole show, only letting go to occasionally dip into our sweets. I wanted to put my arm around her shoulder but not being on the back row and with so many of my friends from school behind me, I thought better of it.

After the film, we retrieved our bikes and cycled on to Victoria Park where we sat on the grass and talked for a while but too soon, I had to leave to go to my Saturday afternoon job at the Campion's house. It seemed that we had both enjoyed our first date together and over the next couple of months we saw each other regularly at weekends, returning to the cinema or Park or meeting at my house to simply ride around on our bikes. Of course, we also saw each other almost every day at school. Although I did eventually get to put my arm around Janet, ours was a pretty innocent relationship, mostly just holding hands with only a few inexperienced, rather stiff kisses fleetingly exchanged. However, it meant a lot to me at the time and I felt a loss when it all finally ended in the summer holidays. For most of August, Janet was away, firstly with her parents at the seaside for two weeks holiday and then with her aunt and uncle in Worcester. Although before she left, we promised each other to meet up again in September, it never happened. By the time Janet returned from her holidays, I had unexpectedly moved to a new home out in Lillington. Naturally she didn't know my new address and although I knew roughly where her house was, I didn't know the exact street. I tried cycling around the area in which I thought she lived one Saturday morning in the hope that I might see her but without success. Since we had both now started at different senior schools, we no longer had any means of direct contact and although for a few weeks I held onto the hope that I might bump into her again somewhere, sadly I never did.

With the arrival of the summer term in 1956 the looming Eleven-Plus exam began to assume more importance in my life. Although I generally enjoyed school, I was not a particularly academic student. At the junior school in Lillington I was in the top set but usually hovering around the middle of the class. I can't remember having a favourite subject and was probably just average at all of them. I did however, show some aptitude during the weekly art and craft classes run by our form master, Mr Fox. He was keen to teach us all cane basket weaving which had become a quite popular national hobby at that time. Over the course of several months I arrived home with a series of cane creations such as baskets for bread or fruit, a set of egg cups and a rather lop-sided waste paper bin. I also enjoyed learning to do chalk and charcoal drawing though I wasn't particularly good at it. Charcoal sticks were cheap to buy at the art shop in town and I used to borrow my mother's tailor's chalk, much to her annoyance when she later tried to find it.

We never had any regular homework at school but in the weeks leading up to the exam we were given some sample test papers during our lessons and I tried to pay close attention to these. Although my mother was ambitious for me and wanted me to go to grammar school, she never pushed me to do any special preparatory work for the exam. She did however, discuss it with me, stressing how important the process was for my future and reminding me how disappointed Dennis was when he failed to pass the previous summer. On the actual day of the exam, I don't recall feeling any pressure or anxiety, even though this was one of the most important days in my life so far. I simply rode my bike to school as normal, took the papers and went home.

Despite my lack of preparation and relaxed approach, I fortunately passed my Eleven-Plus exam and was given the opportunity to go on to grammar school. However, when the results were announced, it turned out that I was a candidate for a place at Warwick School, then regarded as the best of the grammar schools in the area. My mother received the news in a letter inviting me to attend an interview at Warwick a few days later. She clearly did some checking up on the school and their interview process as the morning of the interview she primed me with careful instructions about how to behave and what to say. Most important, she explained, was that the headmaster apparently didn't like TV and thought it was a timewaster for boys who should be studying so, if asked whether I watched it, I should firmly say no. Since I enjoyed children's TV and only a couple of evenings before, the whole family had been fervently gathered around our set to watch the first Eurovision Song contest broadcast from Switzerland, such a response was palpably untrue. However, in the lexicon of human sins, telling a little white lie is not a big thing so neither my mother nor I felt that denying I watched TV was going to be a problem.

At the interview, I thought that I coped well with the various tests and questions thrown at me until, as I was heading for the door, the headmaster casually threw out his question about TV. In an effort to compose my most believable face and voice tone, I hesitated and then turning to face the headmaster, I tried to find the words I had been primed with 'No, I don't watch television'. Instead, what I heard stumbling out of my mouth was 'Well, not really'. It wasn't what I wanted to say, it wasn't what I had been told to say but it was what I said and to this day I don't know why I said it. The combination of my hesitation and my three-word reply were enough for the headmaster to sense blood and I soon found myself admitting that I did watch TV 'occasionally'. Still not the whole truth but apparently enough to seal my fate as a few days later we received a letter of rejection from Warwick School and an offer of a place at Leamington College for Boys instead. Although not as prestigious as Warwick School, it had a good reputation and was based in an impressively large, mock-Tudor style brick building. It was also much easier to get to as it was only round the corner from our flat in Kenilworth Road.

My friends, Richard and Clive also passed their Eleven-Plus exams but evidently managed to handle the TV question better than me and both were offered places at Warwick. Sadly, Barry didn't pass and so went to one of Leamington's secondary schools. During the summer, Andrew's parents had agreed to sell their hotel to the Leamington College for Boys to make way for a major extension at the school and the whole family then moved down south somewhere. In a few short weeks, our 'Famous Five' had been split up and the close friendship of the past couple of years was at an end. If it hadn't been for my 'George Washington' moment of telling the truth, I would at least have gone to senior school with two good friends. As it was, I would have to start my new school without any close friends. I never saw Andrew again but did later bump into Barry once or twice in town but as new horizons had opened up for each of us, we went our separate ways. Some five years later, I also met up again with both Richard and Clive when by coincidence, we all took jobs at the Leamington Post Office as Christmas temporary workers.

Starting my new school not only meant losing good friends once again, it also involved a major outlay by my mother on my new uniform. If I remember correctly, the cost for my new green blazer alone was ten pounds – an impossible expense for us coming as it did at the same time as our unexpected move to a new home in Lillington. My mother wrote immediately to my father in Canada explaining the problem and fortunately, he sent the money needed by return. Then, like many other children before and since, I was kitted out with a slightly oversize blazer so that it would hopefully last for several years. The rest of my outfit, grey shorts and socks, school tie, white shirt and striped green cap plus a pair of boots for rugby were purchased second-hand from various sources in town. Despite the mixed provenance of my school uniform, I felt very smart and proud when I tried everything on for a photo to mail to my father.

Our family move to Lillington came suddenly when in late July 1956, my mother was given notice by our landlord to vacate the flat by the end of August. Apparently, the landlord wanted to redevelop the building into five smaller but more modern flats. This came as a complete shock to my mother as well as Isobel downstairs and the Husseys upstairs. My mother had enough of a struggle working to make ends meet without taking time to now find new, affordable accommodation for the three of us plus Pat and room for Brian as well if he ever showed up again. For a couple of weeks, she frantically chased up the few possibilities advertised in the local paper but without result. There was talk of Pat having to move back to Galley Common to live with Stan and Mary again which Pat adamantly refused to contemplate. In desperation as the days ticked by, my mother mentioned our plight to several of her clients, one of whom was a local councillor. After diligently making enquiries with the Housing Department of the local council, this lady discovered that there were currently a couple of newly-built council houses on an estate in Lillington that had not yet been allocated to anyone. The councillor then organized for my mother to meet with officials at the Housing Department a couple of days later so that she could plead our case. A few days later, much to my mother's relief, she was informed that we would be given one of these vacant houses and could move in the following week. The removal date was set for the morning of September 1st 1956, the day before my twelfth birthday.

Somehow, Isobel managed to agree a delayed departure – I think her lease specified a three-month notice period. Meanwhile, the Husseys managed to find alternative accommodation quite quickly, renting a small two-bedroomed flat on the third floor of a building at the south end of town. When they moved out in late August, I sadly had to say goodbye to Dennis, my long-term friend and partner in so many boyhood adventures and escapades. It was not quite the last I would see of him but it was yet another a definite parting of the ways. We would now be living at opposite ends of the town, some three miles apart and this, together with the fact that we would each be at different schools, meant that our future paths would rarely cross.

The move to Lillington went without a hitch. All our worldly goods were soon loaded into a large removal van which with me riding in the cab and my mother, Fiona and Pat in a taxi, safely delivered us to our brand-new home. At the time, our move to 3, Wellington Road seemed one of the best birthday presents I ever received. It was a new mid-terrace property with three bedrooms, a modern kitchen and bathroom with an immersion heater for hot water plus a fire in the living room with a back boiler that heated a radiator in the kitchen. It also had a small store room for our bikes and a decent sized plot for a garden. No more draughty windows or damp patches on the walls, hot water when we needed it, a garden to play in and no noisy tenants upstairs. The only significant shortcoming of the house was that the room sizes were much smaller than those of our Kenilworth Road flat. As before, I would share the main bedroom with my mother and Fiona but now there was only just enough space to fit both their double and my single bed into the room. The second bedroom served as a bedroom for Brian and a workroom for my mother while Pat occupied the small single bedroom. It was all a little tight but we had managed to stay together as a family and were ready for the next chapter in our lives.

Our change of residence however, did bring one major inconvenience for me. In a perverse twist of fate, our new home in Lillington turned out to be directly opposite the junior school to which I had spent the past three years cycling up and down from Kenilworth Road. I could even see my old classroom across the playing fields from our new bedroom. I would now have to spend the next six years cycling along exactly the same route but now in the reverse direction. Looking back now, that summer of 1956 would prove to be a watershed in all our lives. Although we didn't know it at the time, our mainly happy-go-lucky days at Kenilworth Road would become increasingly difficult and challenging. Despite the fact that my early life there had not always been easy, the occasional problems or moments of sadness were vastly outweighed by memories of childhood happiness, freedom and fun. This sense of well-being owed much to my mother whose sustained and stoic fortitude in the face of adversity was remarkable. So, as I finally left Kenilworth Road, it was with mixed emotions, a feeling of sadness coupled with optimism for the future. Exchanging the hustle and bustle of the centre of Leamington after almost seven years for life on a council estate in Lillington wasn't something I had sought or expected. But perhaps like Marilyn Monroe in her film *The Seven Year Itch*, it was time to move on and explore what new things life had to offer.

Part Two

1956 – 1964

Loves & Labours Lost - and Found

Chapter One
NEW BEGINNINGS

The short journey in the removal van that first day of September to our new home in Lillington was one full of excitement and anticipation. My mother had cycled up there to see it one afternoon a few days before and although she gave us a brief description on her return, none of us knew what it would really be like inside. For me, the chance to ride up front in the brown-painted removal van as we drove to Lillington was an unexpected, added bonus. After twenty minutes or so, we pulled up outside the house in Wellington Road. My mother, Pat and Fiona had already arrived, having travelled there in a taxi. The front door was open and I rushed in and quickly joined my cousin Pat in an initial exploration of the as yet empty house. However, it didn't take long for the two removal men to unload our possessions and under my mother's direction, place them in the appropriate rooms. It was all done within an hour and almost before we knew it, the men were driving off back to Leamington in their now empty Bedford van.

The initial challenge for my mother was to decide how best to sort out the detailed arrangement of our furniture. Both the overall space as well as each individual room in Wellington Road were considerably smaller than at Kenilworth Road. I don't think the word 'downsizing' was in common use then but whatever the equivalent was in the 1950s, that's what we were now doing. Knowing that we would have less room, a couple of days before the move, my mother had sold various items of furniture that would not fit into our new house to one of the second-hand furniture dealers in town. Even so, space was now at a premium, especially in the two main bedrooms upstairs.

The largest bedroom which was to be shared by my mother, Fiona and I was less than half the size of the one we had at Kenilworth Road. Trying to squeeze in a double bed, a dressing table and a large wardrobe for the use of my mother and Fiona plus a single bed and small chest of drawers for my clothes took some time. It was a real struggle for the combined strength of my mother, Pat and I to shift all the furniture around to find a workable combination. In the end, there was just enough room to move between the two beds, as long as you walked sideways. The second bedroom was equally crammed with a single bed and small wardrobe for Brian to use on his visits home plus my mother's sewing machine, work table and a large mahogany chest on chest that contained all her dress-making equipment and materials. Pat had the third, single bedroom, where there was sufficient space for her bed, a wardrobe and an old chest of drawers that also served as a dressing table.

Downstairs, things were much easier and our living room and kitchen were soon in relatively good order. There was food in the pantry, our gas cooker worked, we had hot water from the immersion heater and there were no damp patches or leaks. We had our own gardens at last – a small one to the front and a larger area at the rear – in which I could play any time without being chased off. Beyond the end of our garden fence lay an, as yet, unused plot of land that we later learnt was earmarked for garages for our part of the estate. It all seemed adequate for our needs and by late afternoon, we were finally settled after what had been a very anxious month, especially for my mother.

The Lillington that we arrived in that summer of 1956 was essentially split into two parts. The first was the original village which dated back to before the time of William the Conqueror's Domesday Book but it was only incorporated into Leamington in 1890. The old village contained the pretty parish church of St Mary Magdalene with its pre-Norman origins, an attractive stone manor house (whose owner would later become one of my mother's good clients), plus a few streets of Victorian terraced houses and several small estates of predominantly semi-detached houses built since the 1930s. St Mary's churchyard contained lots of old gravestones in a variety of styles, the most well-known probably being the grave of William Tree who died in 1810 at the fair age of seventy-seven. His weather-beaten headstone bears a terse and rather lugubrious inscription, often quoted in nineteenth-century guides to Leamington:

> "I Poorly Liv'd and Poorly Dy'd,
> Poorly Bury'd and no one Cry'd."

Despite this sad verse, it seemed obvious to me that someone must have cared sufficiently for him to have his memorial stone erected. St Mary's large churchyard was also where my mother was buried after her death in late 1973.

The second area of Lillington which was where we now living was predominantly an immense new council estate. Construction had started in the early 1950s, steadily filling in a large area of former farmland between the old village of Lillington and the Campion Hills to the south with hundreds of homes. The only other noteworthy landmark in the Lillington area was the so-called Midland Oak which sat at the junction of Lillington Avenue and Lillington Road. Reputedly dating from the sixteenth century, it's location supposedly marked the very centre of England. I used to ride by it every day on my bicycle on my way to and from school and it gave me a small sense of pride to think that I lived at the very heart of England. However, as I sadly discovered in later life, there were other locations that lay claim to this prestigious fact, probably with greater scientific justification. Coincidentally, the great oak died in 1967, the year that I finally left Leamington to embark on my working career.

In the 1980s, a replacement tree was subsequently planted, grown from an acorn collected from the original.

There was one other point of interest or perhaps curiosity at that time in Lillington – the couple of rows of 'prefab' houses in Buckley Road on the eastern edge of our council estate. These curious small bungalows, looking very much like a modern-day Portakabin, were designed as a temporary measure to ease the chronic housing shortage at the end of World War II. The project was pushed through by the Prime Minister at the time, Winston Churchill, who originally wanted half a million 'prefabs' built across the country as a stop-gap measure until labour could be mobilised for more permanent housing. As the term implies, these innovative homes were pre-built in sections in factories that had previously been used to make military products such as aeroplanes for the war effort. The finished sections were delivered to site and erected on a pre-laid concrete slab. In some places, prisoners of war who were still being held in Britain were used to help in their construction and I believe this was the case in Lillington. These two-bedroom 'prefabs' could be completed very quickly once the sections were delivered to the site. Unlike traditional houses they came with fully-fitted kitchens and bathrooms and it only took around forty man-hours to assemble them, complete with lighting, plumbing and heating systems.

The first 'prefabs' were completed June 1945 and within a couple of years, more than 150,000 of these miniature homes were erected across the country. They were only expected to last for ten years but they proved very popular with some residents who liked their cosiness and the low rent. Once the new council estates building programme was fully underway, most of the 'prefabs' were demolished but a few remained as in the case of Buckley Road in Leamington. Their occupants liked them and refused to move out into more 'normal' homes. I used to regularly walk by these unique, little box-like homes and along with many others, wondered why people still lived in them. The 'pre-fabs' in Lillington were ultimately demolished to make way for some similar-sized but more modern and durable bungalows. However, a few of these curious homes have survived elsewhere in the country, with over 300 still in use in the city of Bristol.

This radical, post-war, social experiment in re-housing large numbers of people on enormous new council estates, away from their previous social milieu was of course taking place right across the country. Some 900,000 slums were cleared in the 1950s and 1960s and 2.5 million people were re-housed, mostly on large council estates constructed like ours on the periphery of towns and cities. Facilities were often limited on these estates although that was not totally the case in Lillington by the time we arrived. By 1956, the majority of the main phase of building work was complete, although there were some unfinished roads as well as several large empty plots of land, including one to the rear of our terrace. The estate included a new shopping area on Crown Way, my former junior school and its playing fields, an off-licence and later, a community centre and library. The estate also contained three massive tower blocks. Located on the edge of the Campion Hills, the tallest of these, *Eden Court*, dominated the Lillington sky-line and can still be seen for miles outside Leamington. For those who enjoyed a drink or two, the council had even thoughtfully recently completed a large public house – *The Walnut Tree* (now replaced by a supermarket). However, some things were lacking or inadequate. For example, there was no doctor or dentist's surgery on the estate. The bus service into town was very limited and we were miles from the nearest train station and the main centres of employment or social activity in Leamington.

Apart from the infrequent bus service, the other issues were generally not too worrisome for us. But for many residents on these new estates, these kinds of difficulties exacerbated one of the most serious and enduring problems that they had to deal with - a feeling of isolation in their new community. As we would discover, it was a problem that we would also face as we gradually began to e3ncounter our new neighbours. Our Wellington Road house was the middle one of a terrace of three, with the houses on either side being slightly smaller with only two bedrooms. To the right in number 5, was a couple who had moved in some twelve months before. They were about the same age as my mother and lived there with their son who was seventeen or eighteen years old. He left soon after we moved in to join the army so we never really got to know him. The husband and wife both worked so we saw little of them apart from the occasional exchange over the garden fence at weekends. The husband seemed affable enough but I don't think my mother much liked the wife – she was a bottle-blonde (as I heard my mother comment to my cousin Pat one day). She seemed to look down on us and I think the feeling must have been mutual.

The house on the left of ours, number 1, was empty and remained so for several months until Mr and Mrs Grant, a couple in their early thirties, moved in. Our other immediate neighbours across the road were older than my mother with no children at home apart from one couple with two young girls. Apart from an introductory conversation with my mother one day soon after we arrived and the occasional brief nod if we met in the street, I can't recall any of these four families having anything to do with us or anyone else in our street. It was almost as if we didn't exist. As at times in Kenilworth Road, we once again felt isolated and shunned, at least until the Grants moved in next door. On each corner of Wellington Road, where it joined Valley Road, there were a pair of semi-detached bungalows occupied by pensioners. My mother occasionally spoke with one of the elderly residents who as a widow was on her own like my mother but otherwise, there was rarely any interaction by the residents in the other three bungalows with us or any of our neighbours. These pensioners must have led very lonely lives on the estate, relocated here, away from their families and previous friends or neighbours with very little to do – at least until the Community Centre opened a few years later. The relatively small number of pensioners on our estate partly reflected the low life expectancy at that time with few people living much beyond retirement age.[8]

I can't remember now what, if anything, I expected when we moved to Lillington. But I probably had in mind images of what life was like of the streets I knew from our time in Kenilworth Road. They were far from perfect and things didn't always run smoothly but there was definitely a sense of community there (even if we had sometimes been excluded). Although they weren't necessarily close friends, people knew each other and understood something of their neighbours' lives. In Lillington, at least as far as I could see, there was never the kind of neighbourly relationship one might otherwise have expected. Lillington was a location not a community and we lived in houses not homes. Important occasions such as Easter, Bonfire Night, Christmas and New Year all seemed to pass by with little discernible celebration by or within the local community. Although there were often events taking place in Leamington itself, getting to them now involved at least a half hour walk in each direction or a couple of bus rides, if they were running.

In Kenilworth Road when I looked out of our front window, I saw the world go by, day or night. Here, if I looked out of the window, there was definitely no world going by and it just felt as if there was nothing interesting ever happening. The lace-covered windows staring at us in the houses opposite remained as impenetrable as the residents themselves and at times we felt as if we were under some form of lace-curtained surveillance. It is hard to fully convey the sense of isolation and tedium that slowly but surely crept into our lives during our first few months in Lillington. The later hit song '*Little Boxes*' by

---

[8] When I was born in 1944, average life expectancy for a male child was around 63 years. This had risen to 68 by the time I left home in 1964 and the figure now is closer to 80.

Pete Seeger[9] could well have been written about our estate. Of course, this mass re-housing of people on large estates was a new experience for almost everyone involved – the councils, the planners and of course for us, the residents. The social problems were not envisaged or fully understood and it would take time for people to adjust and a sense of community to develop.

Once we had more or less sorted out the interior arrangements in our new house, the next major challenge was to try to tackle the gardens. The one at the front was relatively easy to deal with. It consisted of two small patches of bare soil split into two by a concrete path that led to our front door. As it was our front garden and therefore visible to the neighbours and visiting clients, it was important to my mother that it looked presentable. One weekend, during one of Brian's infrequent visits home, my mother decided that we should turn the bare soil into lawn. She duly purchased a bag of grass seed and following the advice from one of our neighbours, Brian and I dug over and levelled the ground, scattered the seeds and then raked them in. Neither of us really knew what we were doing but it seemed to work and after a few weeks the grass started to appear. With a couple of rose plants bought from Woolworths in town, it actually started to look like a garden. That was the good news. The bad news was that my mother now assigned me the responsibility of regularly cutting the new lawn with a small second hand, rusty push-mower she had bought. In more professional and less begrudging hands, I'm sure the mower could have done an adequate job, especially if it had been oiled and serviced. However, the combination of my unwilling hands and the blunt cutting blades usually resulted in a scene that would have dismayed Percy Thrower.[10] Over

---

[9] The song was a hit in 1963 and is a satire about the development of suburbia and mocks the rows of suburban housing as 'little boxes' which 'all look just the same'.

[10] Percy Thrower became nationally known through presenting various gardening programmes, starting in 1956 on the BBC's Gardening Club.

the ensuing years, the situation was often made worse because I invariably tried to find excuses for not doing the mowing – it was too wet, too cold or I had homework to do. By the time I did get around to it, the grass was often too long for the mower to properly cut, even if it had sharp blades and the end result was an ugly butchering of our little lawn.

The back garden was much more problematic. When we moved in, it was a wild wilderness of weeds that somehow managed to flourish on a mixture of builder's rubble and solid clay soil. When my mother and I first tried to dig and clear the back garden, we found it was impossible to push the spade into the ground more than a few inches at a time. The dry summer months had baked the red Midlands clay rock hard. It was back-breaking work for both of us and our initial enthusiasm for creating a garden soon paled. Even when we had managed to turn over part of the ground, nothing much would grow in the heavy clay soil apart from weeds. Over the next year, we tried a variety of ways to try to break up the solid clumps of clay - chimney soot, builders sand and digging in the weeds to rot down – but without much progress. Our back garden was never much more than a rather sparse lawn (and I use that word loosely) with a few plants donated by a couple of my mother's clients from their own gardens.

Our own little wilderness didn't worry me too much as it provided a great space for me to play in. However, it frustrated my mother as I know she really wanted a pleasant green lawn edged with a couple of flower beds that she could enjoy in the summer. It was all the more annoying as our neighbours in number 5 and later the Grants in number 1 both managed to turn their respective patches of Midland clay into respectable gardens. We just didn't have the strength to cultivate the soil or the money to buy plants. For two successive summers, I did try growing a few vegetables from seeds that Joan and Andrew in Kenilworth gave me. I still continued to visit them occasionally on a Saturday but it was a difficult and costly journey involving two buses each way with a long walk between them. Under Andrew's tutelage, I had previously grown some quite respectable-looking carrots, radishes and French beans in their light sandy soil. Sadly, the results I now obtained in our heavy clay from the packets of seeds that Andrew now gave me were not very successful and I eventually gave up.

Chapter Two
SETTLING INTO OUR NEW LIFE

My mother only kept very limited records or details of her clients so our enforced relocation from Kenilworth Road caused some unwelcome short-term disruption in her business. The lack of notice and doubts about where we would end up, made it doubly difficult to let clients know what was happening. Once it was certain that we were moving to Lillington, my mother and I spent a hectic week cycling around the Leamington area trying to let as many people know our plans. However, as some of her clients came from outside the town and my mother didn't know their exact addresses, it was impossible to contact them – we had no telephone then at our new house. Inevitably, her dress-making business suffered which coming on top of our removal costs and other expenses relating to setting up our new home in Lillington, meant that money was tight for a while. It took around twelve months for things to sort themselves out and by then, my mother was starting to find a few additional new clients in Lillington itself.

Within a few days of our arrival in Lillington, the autumn term started at my new school, the Leamington College for Boys which was housed in an imposing, red-brick Victorian building just around the corner from our former home in Kenilworth Road. The transition from junior school life to that at my new, much larger grammar school was a bigger change than I anticipated. Along with another one hundred or so boys, I was once again a new boy in the first year and rubbing shoulders with sixth form boys who were really young men of seventeen or eighteen. There were several boys I knew from my previous junior school but as luck would have it, we ended up in separate classes and so once again, it was a case of trying to make new friends. My trusty Raleigh bike got me up and down to school for the twenty-minute ride four times each day (I came home for lunch), complete with my brown leather satchel over my shoulder and my new school cap. My very first day did not get off to an auspicious start. During the morning break in the playground, I found myself reluctantly involved in a fight with an older boy from the second year. I can't remember now exactly why he started it but very quickly we were grappling with each other. I managed to land a forceful blow to his face which knocked him over onto the playground tarmac. Fortunately, that took the wind out of him and when he got up, he sheepishly retreated to another part of the playground. It was a rumbustious start to my grammar school days but I'm glad to say that things were much quieter after that – at least for a few years.

That summer of 1956 also marked an important milestone for my cousin Pat. She was now approaching sixteen and had come to the end of her school-days at Milverton. Her full-time presence in our new home was initially a benefit for my mother as we settled in. But soon, the inevitable restlessness of a lively, fun-loving teenager caused tensions. Pat was far from happy being stuck on a council estate away from the centre of Leaminton. She still had her Saturday job in town which gave her enough pocket money for make-up, girls magazines and the odd night out but there was nothing to do in Lillington. She was bored and ended up moodily moping around the house. Both Pat and my mother soon became fed up with the situation and agreed that Pat should find a full-time job as soon as possible. With no skills or training, this was easier said than done. However, after a couple of months of searching, Pat eventually found work as a shop assistant in the newsagents in the nearby Crown Way shopping arcade.

As with many youngsters starting their first job, Pat found the transition from school life to full-time work difficult. But to her credit, she stuck at it. My mother was happy that Pat now had something to occupy her time but I also appreciated the benefits that her new job brought. She was generous when weighing out the loose sweets that I occasionally bought on Saturday mornings and sometimes she would bring home a Beano or Dandy comic for me. Pat was much happier now that she had some money to finance a more active social programme. With her lively personality, she also enjoyed chatting to the many people she met in the shop, especially the young men. Within weeks of her starting the job, we began to see a stream of these young men calling at our house in the evenings and at weekends asking to speak to Pat. However, not all of her visitors turned out to be young.

After about a year, it was clear to my mother that Pat now had a regular boyfriend from Leamington and since she was only seventeen, my mother was protectively curious about this new relationship. Pat normally caught the bus into town to meet him but one Saturday night, he called at our house to collect her. When he knocked at the front door, Pat was upstairs in her bedroom getting ready so my mother went to answer it. I was watching TV in the living room and soon heard Pat rushing downstairs and then the sounds of raised voices and a scuffle in the front hall. Curious, I went to see what was going on. My mother had hold of the man's arm and was trying to push him out of the front door. The man was shouting at my mother and Pat was screaming, almost in tears. It tuned out that when my mother had opened the front door, she became suspicious when she saw that Pat's boyfriend had arrived in a smart car and was obviously much older than Pat. Her doubts were confirmed when under 'interrogation' he told my mother that he was twenty-six. An argument had ensued about his intentions and suitability for Pat and then despite the protests of her aspiring boyfriend, I witnessed him finally being ejected onto the front path as my mother shouted at him 'and don't come back, she's far too young for you.'

Like many a teenager before her, Pat was distraught and inconsolable for several days but eventually agreed that my mother was right. Time passed, her broken heart mended and a few months later, she was going steady with a young man from Kenilworth called Jim Gregory. Jim became an increasingly frequent weekend visitor at our house and I grew to like him, as did my mother. He was quiet but with an easy-going nature with a good sense of humour and worked in the building trade. My mother reckoned that if he was willing to make the lengthy bus journey from Kenilworth to Lillington, he must be have had real affection for Pat. He often arrived with a few bottles of beer that he purchased from the off-licence at the end of Valley Road which my mother, Pat and Jim then consumed while watching TV or playing cards. I enjoyed his visits as they enlivened our otherwise rather dull routine and he made my mother laugh which was always good to see. Some six months later Pat and Jim became engaged and they eventually married in 1959, moving into a small terraced house in Kenilworth to start their married life together.

After Brian left home to join the Royal Navy, we rarely saw or heard from him. He returned to Wellington Road for a couple of short visits during his initial training and we subsequently received occasional postcards from exotic places like Aden and Hong Kong while he was away at sea. When he eventually came home on leave after his first overseas tour of duty in the summer of 1958, he was a different person in several ways. His time so far in the Navy had made him tougher, both physically and mentally. He was no longer the rather weedy teenager who had left home in 1956. He also had money to spend and was out on the town most nights during his home leave. One Saturday afternoon, I went shopping with him into Leamington and as we walked down The Parade, he suddenly pulled out a crisp, ten-shilling note from his wallet and thrust it onto my hand saying I should have some fun and spend it. I was completely taken aback by his wholly unexpected generosity and initially unsure what to do with my new-found wealth but a little while later, when I followed Brian into a record store, I knew what I wanted. While Brian bought himself a portable Bush record player, I purchased my very first record, a 78rpm of Tommy Steele's *'Singing the Blues'* which had recently topped the UK singles chart. When Brian went back to sea after his 1958 visit, he left behind his record player and record collection with stern instructions that it wasn't to be touched. Of course, Pat and I ignored this and regularly used his record player to entertain ourselves. Brain's records by Nat King Cole and Frank Sinatra were a bit old fashioned for us but Pat gradually added a few, more modern records and I could listen to Tommy Steele.

As that summer of '56 inexorably faded into autumn, life continued much as it had in Kenilworth Road. I went to school each weekday, my mother sewed, cleaned and cooked while Fiona generally sat and played by herself or watched TV. I still regularly delivered my mother's dressmaking output on my bike in the evenings and at weekends only now it took much longer to get to most clients than before. I remained in the choir at Holy Trinity Church in Beauchamp Avenue, at least until my voice broke a year or so later and the Rev Anstey still called in to see us occasionally. The TV was our only source of entertainment and we watched it together almost every night. Along with millions of other families across the UK, listening to the radio still remained popular, especially on Sunday mornings while preparing and eating lunch. The BBC Light programme schedule of the morning service, *Round the Horne* and *Forces Favourites* was a permanent fixture in our lives in those days. Our eating habits and diet also stayed largely unchanged although there were no longer the occasional delicious treats from Elizabeth's cake shop or the deli in Burgis & Colbourne. Our Sunday lunch and subsequent week-day meals, were invariably derived from a leg of New Zealand lamb that I collected from the local butcher each Saturday morning. We continued to receive (and appreciate) the annual shipment of butter at Christmas from Aunt Laurie in New Zealand. My weekly bath routine on Saturday evenings also remained unchanged but it was a much easier affair than the previous struggle with the old gas-fired geyser at Kenilworth Road.

There were a few changes however. We no longer went to the Victoria Park in Leamington on Sunday afternoons in summer. Fiona was now too big to ride on the back of my mother's bike and it was too far away to walk. There were no equivalent public parks or gardens in Lillington. The nearest open space was the Campion Hills but although the views across Leamington were impressive, there were no amenities or ice-dream kiosks as in Victoria Park. Such things were far more important then for a youngster like me. Anyway, now that we had our own garden, there was less need to go out to a park. I'm also glad to say that the other good change (at least for me) was that we no longer attended the British-Israelites Society meetings in Leamington; it was now too difficult to attend their mid-week evening sessions. As a result of the fact that my mother, Fiona and I were now sharing the one bedroom, a new tradition gradually evolved. Once we were all in bed, my mother would often ask me to sing to her to help her go to sleep. I didn't know many songs by heart so it was usually a hymn or her favourite, the Skye boat song. My mother enjoyed the sound of singing and she once told me that she had done a little operatic training when she was young. I think she had a fine voice but she never joined in my singing. Indeed, she rarely relaxed or let herself go which I'm sure was a barrier to her making close friends.

Our overall health generally remained good too. The main exception was our involuntary participation in the Asian 'flu epidemic that swept the country in late 1957. Pat was hit first, then my mother and Fiona the following day with me finally succumbing twenty-four hours later. The virus attacked quickly and the symptoms were extremely debilitating with wobbly legs and a chill followed by a sore throat, running nose and cough, together with aching limbs and a high fever. We were all soon confined to bed and virtually unable to move or do anything in the house for around a week. Too ill to go out to telephone the doctor or walk to the chemists to buy medicine, the four of us survived on a diet of aspirins and a bottle of cough medicine that we already had at home plus copious cups of tea. We got off relatively lightly. By early 1958, it was estimated that more than nine million people in Great Britain had contracted the virus and around 14 000 people died of the immediate effects of their attack. Hospital wards were closed across the country as the nurses and doctors fell ill and many factories, schools, offices and mines closed, causing a significant dip in economic output. Similar impacts were felt in many other countries as the epidemic's relentless rampage spread across the globe's northern hemisphere during the winter of 1957/58. In the USA alone, some 70,000 deaths were attributed to Asian 'flu.

I missed having my previous nearby circle of friends to play with, especially Dennis and I increasingly felt somewhat bereft and a little lonely. As luck would have it, the couple of new friends I had made at school both lived in Whitnash, a suburb on the south side of Leamington and it simply wasn't practical to meet up regularly after school or at weekends. We did go to visit the Hussey family one Sunday afternoon for tea in their new flat at the south end of Leamington and it was good to see Dennis again. Mr Hussey was his usual charming self and Mrs Hussey told my mother that her husband was not drinking as much as before and so things were now better between the two of them. Although I didn't know it at the time, this was to be last occasion I would see Dennis. Travelling across Leamington to visit them wasn't an easy journey, especially with Fiona and we never went again although Mrs Hussey did come to see us occasionally in Lillington in later years.

The lack of any friendly neighbours improved somewhat for us when in the spring of 1957, the Grants moved into the empty house next door. They had just returned to England from Kenya where Mr Grant had been working for several years as a public health inspector. He had now taken a job with the local council in the same line of work and his wife worked as a nurse. They were allocated the house by the council as a temporary measure until they could find a permanent local home. Although initially, they didn't seem very happy about living on a council estate, they ended up staying next door for several years. I would like to think that the reason was that the Grants enjoyed having us as neighbours but as they later explained to my mother, the real explanation was financial. Their extended stay at a relatively low rent meant that they would eventually be able to save enough money to buy a new house instead of their original plan of renting somewhere.

In a completely fair world, such advantageous perks would not of course be allowed. As the original concept behind these council homes was to provide a place to rent for those who couldn't afford rents in the commercial sector, the Grants clearly didn't qualify. Our new neighbours not only benefitted financially from this arrangement but were in effect displacing a much needier family on the council housing waiting list. But of course, we didn't live in a perfect world and as far as I can remember, this was the first time I came to realize that some people get lucky and gain unfair advantages in life that others don't have. Naturally, we had no room to comment as we had jumped the same waiting list through the fortunate intervention of a councillor, even if we were a more deserving case. However, the Grants proved to be good neighbours to us and became the only friends we had in the street. They invited my mother around occasionally for dinner or a drink at Christmas and were always friendly towards me. As Mr Grant's job involved inspecting local restaurants and food preparation premises, he often had some interesting stories to tell about the places he visited in the course of his work. These usually involved various stomach-churning details about examples of poor hygiene and unsuitable premises. Fortunately, since we couldn't afford to eat out, the potential horrors of Leamington's food scene were no threat to us. Later, after their first child was born, both Pat and I would occasionally baby-sit for them. I soon found out that Mr Grant and I also shared a common interest in stamp collecting and although my collection was minuscule compared to his, we occasionally compared our albums and swapped stamps.

Chapter Three
YOU'VE NEVER HAD IT SO GOOD

In complete contrast to the message behind Tommy Steele's hit record, '*Singing the Blues*' which I had bought a few months earlier, was the famous pronouncement by the Conservative Prime Minister at the time, Harold Macmillan, that 'You've never had it so good.' He was referring to the strong economy, steadily rising living standards and growing consumer boom in the UK for which the Conservatives naturally wanted to take the credit. Although his statement was inevitably hotly debated at the time, he may have had a point. In a recent study[11], academics compiled a UK happiness index covering the last 240 years which showed that the 1950s marked a modern high point in the happiness of the nation. Although this may accurately reflect how many people the country felt at the time, it certainly didn't catch the general mood in our Lillington household during 1956 and 1957. However, over the next couple of years, life did gradually become somewhat better for us so perhaps Macmillan was just a little premature in our case.

One small, unexpected improvement in our everyday lives that did occur around this time resulted from a letter my mother received one day from the council. It was offering us the chance to buy a refrigerator for our house by paying an additional small amount on our weekly rent. I think the deal was an extra two shillings a week over three years which was very reasonable and my mother immediately signed up. Our refrigerator arrived a couple of weeks later and although it was small by today's

---

[11] Published in 2016 by the University of Warwick, the study covered the UK, USA, France, Germany, Italy and Spain.

standards, we could at last keep food fresh, milk cool and enjoy ice in our summer drinks. Around the same time, we also upgraded our TV to a larger model (still black and white), and a year or so later, I had saved up enough money to buy myself a new pocket-sized transistor radio. Although we didn't yet own a telephone or a car (we finally acquired both of these items when I was sixteen), we were slowly but surely joining in the consumer boom that was steadily sweeping the country in the late 1950s, largely fuelled by the rise in real wages and a massive increase in consumer credit.

The most visible sign of the rising incomes and living standards on our estate was the gradual rise in the number of cars that started to appear outside our neighbour's homes. The Grants and the unfriendly couple at number 5 were the first proud car owners, followed a year or two later by each of the neighbours across the street. What happened at our end of Wellington Road was mirrored across the estate and indeed in most other large council estates in the UK. This inexorable increase in vehicle ownership was a phenomenon that the council planners had not allowed for in designing these new housing developments. Most of our streets were relatively narrow, none of the houses had garages and at first, there was virtually no off-street parking available. Since our end of the estate was still being developed, the council was eventually able to build a few garages for rent on the unused land behind our terrace and subsequently, a larger number behind the shopping precinct in Crown Way. Although this improved the parking situation in our immediate area, vehicle congestion remained a problem elsewhere on the estate.

For my mother, the first two years in Wellington Road proved to be especially difficult. I don't know how she managed to pay all the bills for our family of four. Pat made a small contribution towards her upkeep out of her small earnings from the newsagent and my mother received eight shillings (forty pence today) per week in child allowance for Fiona and me. I still over part of my earnings from the choir and carol singing at Christmas but it wasn't much and money was always tight. Although it now was easier to keep Fiona inside than at Kenilworth Road as we had our own front door and a lock on the back-garden gate, my mother was still largely tied to the house the whole day because of the need to take care of Fiona. Also, without any friendly neighbours to chat to during the day, she was mostly alone. Of course, her dressmaking clients came to the house regularly and occasionally one of her car-owning acquaintances from Leamington might pop in for tea but she was still largely stuck in the house. Apart from the loneliness, her main problem was being unable to get out to the shops to buy the items she regularly needed for her business – material, thread, zips, buttons etc. Often, when I arrived back home from school, my mother would tell me my tea was on the table as she zoomed off on her bike into town to buy some urgently-needed supplies or visit one of her clients.

As my mother steadily rebuilt her dressmaking business following our relocation to Lillington, inevitably, more and more clients arrived at our house for fittings and alterations. This was fine during the day but many preferred to come in the evenings or weekends and as I was now a growing teenager, this presented a problem. Although my mother had a folding screen in our living room behind which the women could change, it was somewhat awkward with me sitting on the couch just a few feet away. So, I increasingly found myself banished to the kitchen for twenty or thirty minutes while these client visits took place. All very well during the summer but on winter evenings it was frustrating to have to sit in the cold kitchen for half an hour, especially if the women arrived during one of my favourite TV programmes. Eventually, as I grew older and watched less TV and had more homework, I learned to appreciate these enforced periods in the kitchen as a quiet time to study.

One morning in 1958, as I was heading off to school, I noticed several women and children who I had never seen before waiting on the corner of our street. As I rode by, a minibus pulled up, loaded up all the children and then drove off down Valley Road. I could clearly see that each of the four children had Downs syndrome like Fiona. That evening, I told my mother what I had seen and the next morning she went to investigate. She chatted to the three mothers who told her that the minibus was taking their children to a newly-opened occupational centre for the mentally handicapped in Warwick run by the council. This was encouraging news and within a few days, my mother had registered Fiona with the council so that she could join the other children on the minibus. The centre operated Monday to Friday year-round, apart from Bank Holidays and was free. For my mother, it was a god-send that would change her life. She now had some freedom and time to herself. She also made friends with one of the other mothers – a Dutch woman who sadly had two Downs syndrome girls – which gave my mother someone with whom to share the worries and burdens of looking after a Downs syndrome child.

Around the same time, another development occurred that was to have a significant influence on our lives. My mother started doing dress-making work for a Mrs Elgood who lived in a pleasant Victorian detached house at one end of Beauchamp Avenue. She and her husband, a senior doctor at the local hospital had two children, Robert who was a couple of years younger than me and his younger sister Mary. Despite the fact that my mother was some ten years older than Mrs Elgood, the pair gradually became good friends. Mrs Elgood was an extremely nice and generous person and I think she sympathised with my mother's difficult life. It was also evident to me that my mother increasingly valued this new friendship. We were invited round to the Elgood's home for tea a couple of times and from this I soon developed a close friendship with their son, Robert. Although he was away at boarding school during term time, when he was at home in the holidays, I became an increasingly regular visitor at their house. We often played cards together with Mary and Robert's father as well as quite an array of board games such as Monopoly and Cluedo. Our particular favourites were conquest board games like Risk, Battleships or Tactics and Robert and I spent many happy hours together playing these. Robert and I also shared other interests such as stamp collecting and reading the same kind of books – adventure stories by Rider Haggard were the ones we enjoyed most.

Dr Elgood was an extremely keen fisherman and used to make all his own flies in an extensive workshop that he had in their basement. He took Robert and me coarse fishing with him a few times. I can still remember the thrill of catching my very first fish – it was probably only a few inches long but that didn't lessen the sudden excitement of that moment. For my birthday that year, Dr Elgood very kindly bought me my own rod and tackle and for a while I used to cycle off for the day to fish in the River Leam. Maybe I failed to pick the right spots or perhaps I just wasn't very good because I never seemed to catch anything but tiddlers. I also found fishing too quiet and sedate; as a fifteen-year-old, I wanted to do things with friends that were more active.

In the summer of 1959, the Elgoods rented an old thatched cottage in the small village of Hogs Norton (now called Hook Norton) in the Cotswolds for a few days and they very kindly invited me to join them. I enjoyed my short holiday with the Elgoods immensely. We were fortunate to enjoy fine, sunny weather and I fell in love with the Cotswolds then and have gladly returned many times since. During the day, Robert, Mary and I had a wonderful time, wandering around the quiet village lanes and out into the surrounding empty countryside. Dr Elgood also took us out in his car a few times; we visited

Blenheim Palace, the Rollright Stones[12] and went to Marlborough for dinner in a posh restaurant with the Elgood's aunt (see story on page 87 of Part One). Each evening, after dinner in the cottage, we sat and talked or played games until bedtime. The many happy hours that I spent with the Elgood family, both in the Cotswolds and more generally at their home in Leamington, became an important point of reference for me. I experienced something of how a normal family functioned and the relationship between a happily married couple. I watched, listened and learned a lot about relationships, how to behave and even how to expand my vocabulary. In a way, they became a role model family for me. I still remember how one sunny evening after dinner in our Cotswold cottage, Dr and Mrs Elgood went out for a walk. I watched them through the kitchen window as they ambled down the lane, holding hands and kissing. I had never witnessed affection like this between a husband and wife. Inevitably, it made me think about my own parents and their failed marriage; I briefly wondered how things might have turned out if our family had still been together.

As far as I can recall, I was the only boy in my year at school from a single-parent family which is surprising given the number of British adults killed during World War II. However, even though I was an exception, I can't remember it having any significant impact on the attitudes of either my classmates or the teachers. Of course, there were a few occasions when I missed having my father around such as parent's evenings, sports days and school plays (in which I often participated). This situation was exacerbated by my mother's inability to attend most of these types of events, either due to her work or being unable to leave Fiona alone at home. Overall though, being from a single-parent family had no apparent effect on me; I was used to it and even if I wanted to change my

---

[12] The Rollright Stones are part of a complex of three Neolithic and Bronze Age monuments on the borders of Oxfordshire and Warwickshire that date back over 4,000 years.

situation, there was nothing I could do about it. Also, as far as I was aware for the first couple of years, I was the only boy from our council estate who attended the grammar school in Leamington. However, in the third form I did come across another boy who as it turned out, lived just a couple of hundred yards away from me. I had just left home on my bike, heading into Leamington to deliver one of my mother's newly finished dresses after school when to my surprise, I saw a boy I vaguely recognized coming out of a house. He was in a different class from me so I didn't know his name but as I cycled by, I shouted 'Hello' to him. He looked blankly at me and failed to respond so I turned my bike around and went back to speak him. Since we were both in our school uniforms, there should have been no doubt that we were fellow pupils. Happy at last to have found someone from the same school and year as me, I started to introduce myself and asked him if he recognized me but as I talked, the other boy seemed to be embarrassed and uncomfortable, mostly staring down at the ground. After a quick glance towards his house, he said to me in what was virtually a whisper that yes, he had seen m around but his family were Plymouth Brethren and he wasn't allowed to talk to me. With that discouraging remark, he turned and immediately walked straight back into his house. After that, although I saw him occasionally at both school and in the neighbourhood, we never spoke to each other again.

As my friendship with my two friends from Whitnash developed during my second and third years at school, I was invited to their respective birthday parties each year. They were not big affairs, usually just three or four boys invited for tea on a Saturday, followed by a game of soccer or French cricket in the garden afterwards. At one of these parties, just as we were sitting down to enjoy the fine tea spread out before us, the birthday boy's mother casually asked me if I was OK. Since it was a hot summer's day and I had cycled the long journey from Lillington to Whitnash, I was feeling rather weary and probably looking a bit red-faced and sweaty. I said that yes, I was a bit hot and please could I have a glass of water. Then, using a word that I had recently heard Jim, Pat's fiancée say that I quite liked the sound of, I explained that I was 'knackered'. The derivation of this term[13] was unknown to me and although it is perhaps in more common use today, at that time it was regarded as very loose slang. The previously benign smile on the face of my friend's mother instantly disappeared, replaced by a look of disbelief and displeasure. In the silence that then followed, if the proverbial pin had been dropped, we all would have heard it clearly.

Whether my friends all knew the meaning of the word I had uttered or not I don't know. But taking their cue from the mother, they each looked at me as if I had suddenly grown devil's horns and I realised that there was more to that word than I knew. After what seemed like hours but was probably just a few seconds, my friend's mother said 'Oh' and abruptly retreated to the kitchen with her husband. For a while, as we boys then tucked into our tea-time spread, we could vaguely hear occasional phrases emanating from the parents in the kitchen along the lines of 'Disgraceful language' and 'Where did he pick up that word?' I felt acutely embarrassed but then my friends around the table started to giggle and the awkward moment passed. But for the rest of the meal, I half-expected the mother to re-appear with a glass of water and tell me to wash out my mouth. I promised myself there and then never to use a word of which I didn't fully understand the meaning.

Having been invited to several of my school friends' birthday parties, I eventually suggested to my mother that I really ought to hold one of my own. Until then, I had never had a proper birthday celebration with my friends invited for tea. In our household, birthdays seemed to come and

---

[13] A knacker refers to someone who disposes of animal corpses, usually those unfit for human consumption. The plural 'knackers' can also mean a man's testicles.

go without much ceremony. We always gave each other cards and usually there was a small present but none of us ever had a party. My mother was a little reluctant at first but eventually came around and so, one Saturday in September 1958, soon after the autumn term started, I invited three friends to my very first birthday party tea. The father of one of the boys kindly agreed to bring them out to Lillington in his car. My mother organised all the necessary sandwiches and cake for us plus the most important element of all – a box of Cadbury's chocolate fingers. For some reason that I can't now remember, these had become something of a tradition at our parties and no event was complete without them. Fortunately, the party went smoothly and there were no embarrassing incidents like my 'faux pas' earlier in the year. Although the day went well, it turned out to be the one and only birthday party I had while living at home.

As mentioned earlier, I continued to sing in the choir at Holy Trinity church until my voice broke. On Sunday mornings, I cycled into Leamington for the matins service but as my mother usually came to the evening service, we would walk to church together with Fiona and back again. It was a good half hour walk each way using the shortest route which took us past the old brickworks where I used to play with Brian and along a path through some allotments along the edge of the Campion Hills. This was alright in the summer months but on a dark, winter's night, the short walk through the silent, unlit allotments was quite scary. We rarely spoke on that part of the journey, our eyes and ears nervously alert for the slightest movement or sound from the surrounding hedges and gardens. Of course, nothing ever happened and we always emerged safely into the bright street lights at the other end, arriving home in time to watch the Sunday evening play on BBC TV.

These evening walks home from church which usually took around half an hour, were one of few times that my mother and I really got to talk to each other. The little I know about my mother's history and that of our wider family as well as her views and feelings was mostly garnered during these Sunday evening journeys. It was during these walks home that I heard about her previous marriage, her first child, stories about our life in Canada and her early family life. Shortly before my voice broke and I left the choir, my mother told me one Sunday evening on the way home that she was not going to attend church any more. I was extremely surprised and shocked to hear this news as I knew my mother had always been strongly religious. Apparently, she had recently raised the subject with our church about her wish to take Holy Communion and was concerned at the Church of England's policy of the time forbidding divorced people from communion. They could attend the service and receive a blessing but couldn't actually take bread and wine. That evening, after the service, the vicar had confirmed to my mother that he had taken advice and she was definitely not allowed to participate. My mother was clearly upset at this news and felt very bitter about the unfairness of this unwelcome decision. Given the situation, she understandably concluded she could no longer attend church and that evening was the very last time she went. I think she still believed in God and she continued to pray with the Rev Anstey on his occasional visits to our Lillington home. However, this sad and unnecessary loss of the church in her life undoubtedly left a gap and was a blow from an institution that should have been more caring and welcoming.

In the summer of 1959, when Pat married her boyfriend Jim and became Mrs Gregory, they moved into a small Victorian terraced house in Kenilworth. It was basically a two-up, two-down home but Jim's building skills soon made it a comfortable place in which to start their family life together. Pat naturally had to give up her job at the newsagent in Crown Way, much to my regret as I now lost my source of free comics and sweets. However, this was more than made up for by the fact after she left, I moved into her former room and for a few short months, I was able to enjoy a bedroom of my own. I now had a place to play games and work on my stamp collection in the evenings as well as to do my school homework plus somewhere to store my things out of reach of Fiona's enquiring fingers. For a while, my mother, Fiona and I occasionally went over to visit Pat and Jim for Sunday lunch but Pat was such an awful cook that I dreaded these trips. Eventually, after pleading with my mother, these occasional visits were reversed so that Pat and Jim came to see us for tea.

A few weeks after Pat and Jim's wedding, Brian came home one weekend for another of his periodical short visits. We hadn't seen or heard from him for perhaps more than a year when out of the blue, he arrived at our doorstep. However, this time he wasn't alone as he had brought with him his new fiancée and told us he was getting married in a few weeks' time. It seemed marriage fever was suddenly all the rage in our family. Brian's fiancée was called Pamela and she was from the Birmingham area with a broad 'Brummy' accent. She was blonde with a good, trim figure, slightly taller than Brian and had just turned eighteen. She seemed a pleasant enough young woman but very quiet and she said little during her visit. I had the impression from my mother that if she did actually say anything, it was unlikely to be of any consequence. To be fair to Pamela, things did not go well during that weekend. Firstly, since none of us knew that Brian had become engaged, it was quite a shock for my mother to find the pair of them on the doorstep. She was clearly annoyed that Brian hadn't told her about his engagement or pre-warn her of their intended visit. We had little food in the house and there was the question of where Pamela would sleep. My mother was adamant that they couldn't share the bed in my mother's work-room that was kept for Brian's occasional trips back home. So inevitably, I had to give up my newly acquired bedroom to

Pamela and move back in with my mother and Fiona for the weekend – I was not pleased.

Secondly, there was the incident of blood on the bed sheets during the first night. I had got up the next morning, had a plate of cereal for my breakfast as usual and gone out to play in the garden. Sometime around mid-morning, it was clear that Brian and his fiancée were now finally up as I could hear voices coming from the kitchen. However, the voices suddenly became louder and I could now hear my mother shouting so I went inside to see what was going on. As I entered the kitchen, I caught sight of Brian and Pamela going upstairs with a bucket of soapy water and some old towels. Then my mother rushed past me carrying some folded-up bed linen and what looked like a nightdress, all of which she thrust into the sink. I asked my mother what was happening but my polite enquiry was studiously ignored as she energetically began to wash the sheets. I wandered upstairs to investigate and found Brian and Pamela hard at work in my bedroom scrubbing down a large bloodstain on my mattress. Somewhat sheepishly, Brian told me that Pamela had had an accident last night – her period had started. I wasn't terribly sure what a period was exactly, although I had heard my mother and Pat talking about it once. I muttered a non-committal reply such as 'Oh, OK' and wandered off back into the garden.

The remainder of the weekend was very tense and my mother was clearly in a bad mood and annoyed. After Brian and Pamela had finally left to return to Birmingham, my mother eventually opened up about the incident. Apparently, Pamela had arrived without any sanitary towels which my mother thought was very careless and her period bleeding during the night had stained my sheets and mattress. The sheets would have to be replaced which was something of an unscheduled expense but we couldn't afford a new mattress. Coming on top of the unannounced visit, engagement and impending wedding, it was all too much for my mother. Poor Pamela never really got a chance to get to know us and my mother and Brian parted on bad terms. The wedding duly took place somewhere in Birmingham a few weeks later but we didn't attend. My mother claimed with some justification that it was too difficult and expensive for us to travel there and back in a day. We never saw or heard from Brian or Pamela again while we lived in Lillington, although my cousin Pat did stay in touch with them intermittently. She later told us that Brian had left the navy and taken a job in Birmingham but sadly, their marriage didn't last and within a few years, they were divorced. Apparently, Pamela had left Brian for another man. Fortunately, they hadn't had any children. I felt sorry for Brian, he had not had an easy life and didn't deserve this. I believe almost everyone is born with the intrinsic ability to do good and contribute to society, if given the chance. Sadly, in Brian's case, there were just too many negative factors combined against him.

At some stage around this time, I volunteered to help look after the school lost property office. It was run from quite a large room, perhaps twelve feet by fourteen with sets of wooden racks running around the walls. On these lay a fascinating mixture of lost or abandoned property that contained most of the paraphernalia needed by boys at our school. It was mostly clothing in all shapes and sizes but also included sporting equipment, satchels, pens and drawing sets plus a few items whose scholastic purpose was far from clear. Of course, everyone at school was told to clearly mark their personal items with their names but evidently, there were plenty of mothers (or fathers) who neglected to do so. The lost and found office was opened up every morning break plus half an hour at lunchtimes and was manned on a rota by myself with two other boys. Any lost property was brought to our office and then if not claimed by the end of term, most items were disposed of by the school caretaker. Over the two years that I did this job, I was staggered to find that so much stuff remained abandoned and unclaimed each term.

I can't recall what my original motive was for volunteering but I soon discovered that it gave me access to all the things I needed but couldn't afford. At the end of each term, before the caretaker cleaned out our office, I was able to help myself to anything due to be removed. As I grew out of my gym pumps, here was a source for replacements. When I needed boots to play hockey, there was a wide selection to choose from and when I lost my school cap it was easy to find another. This was recycling with a personal touch. As I soon discovered, the other two boys that I worked with turned out to be interesting characters. They were both skivers who used the lost property office as a hideaway, either for smoking cigarettes or for betting on the horses. The pair used to regularly arrive in the office with a copy of a racing paper and then sit there deciding on which horses in which races they were going to bet on (I think they were helped in placing their bets by an older brother). They seemed to do moderately well but then most gamblers only tend to talk about the wins and not the losses. They asked me if I wanted to join their syndicate but as I never quite followed the intricacies of doubles and trebles betting and had no money anyway, I declined their offer. Both boys left to start work in the fifth year with no qualifications and I just hope they found some kind of worthwhile career, despite their wasted time at school.

3, Wellington Road

Leamington College for Boys

to all the things I needed but couldn't afford. At the end of each term, before the caretaker cleaned out our office, I was able to help myself to anything due to be removed. As I grew out of my gym pumps, here was a source for replacements. When I needed boots to play hockey, there was a wide selection to choose from and when I lost my school cap it was easy to find another. This was recycling with a personal touch. As I soon discovered, the other two boys that I worked with turned out to be interesting characters. They were both skivers who used the lost property office as a hideaway, either for smoking cigarettes or for betting on the horses. The pair used to regularly arrive in the office with a copy of a racing paper and then sit there deciding on which horses in which races they were going to bet on (I think they were helped in placing their bets by an older brother). They seemed to do moderately well but then most gamblers only tend to talk about the wins and not the losses. They asked me if I wanted to join their syndicate but as I never quite followed the intricacies of doubles and trebles betting and had no money anyway, I declined their offer. Both boys left to start work in the fifth year with no qualifications and I just hope they found some kind of worthwhile career, despite their wasted time at school.

3, Wellington Road

Leamington College for Boys

Pre-fab homes in Lillington

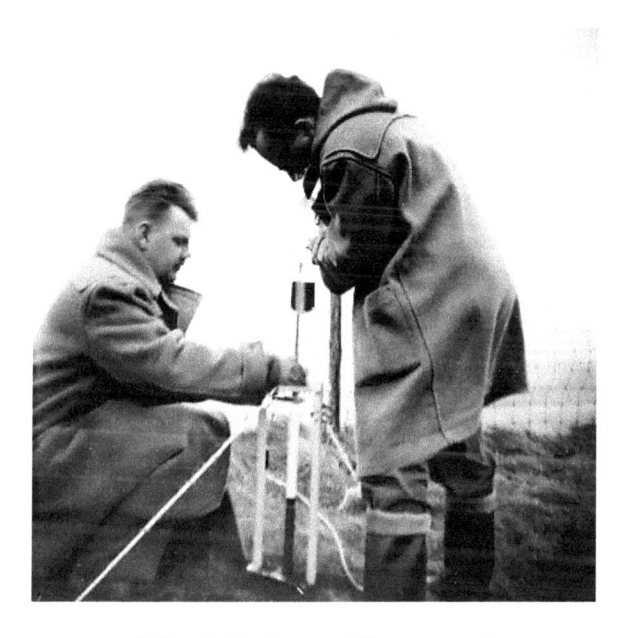

Mike & Prof assembling our rocket

**My father in Florida
1959**

**My mother & Fiona
with our Isetta**

Claudine in St Nazaire, 1963

**Grandmother Eileen & Aunt Bonnie-Jean,
Toronto**

Mother & son, San Sebastian, Spain

Calais docks, returning from Spain, 1964

Chapter Four
ROCKET MAN

After the trauma of Brian and Pamela's visit, I happily re-occupied my bedroom. But my joy was unfortunately short-lived. Some two or three months later, my mother announced one day that my great grandmother, Gran, would be coming to live with us again and would take over my bedroom. I can't recall what, if any, reasons were given at the time for Gran returning to live with us but I was definitely annoyed at having to relinquish my bedroom. I had just turned fifteen and sharing a bedroom with my mother and sister again was far from ideal for any of us. Gran seemed to have aged a lot since she last lived with us in Kenilworth Road. Her pernicious anaemia was much worse and she could only walk with the aid of a stick and even then, not very far. Sadly, her former sense of humour seemed to have waned and she no longer told the little stories or jokes that she did before. I think Gran had also put on weight as pushing her around in the wheelchair now seemed harder than before, even though I was a couple of years older and stronger. Because of her age and health issues, she really couldn't do much, other than sit in a chair and watch TV. At weekends, however, there was an old age pensioner's session at the recently-constructed local community centre and I used to push her round there in her wheelchair, leave her for two hours and then go and collect her.

Gran was fond of an occasional drink, especially at weekends and on a Saturday night, I was often dispatched to the local off-licence to buy something for her. Her favourites were either a bottle of cheap cream sherry which she would share with my mother, or a couple of bottles of stout. She also always gave me enough money to buy a bottle of lemonade and some crisps for myself and Fiona. Gran also liked knitting to while away the hours and during the time she was with us. Although much of her output was not exactly fashionable, for Pat and I, it was a case of grin and wear it. Gran also taught both Fiona and I how to knit. Once Fiona had mastered the basics, she became an addict and spent a large part of each day knitting square after square of brightly coloured wool – usually red or pink. There was nothing we could do with these squares, they just mounted up until my mother had a clear-out and then Fiona started all over again.

Gran's second stay with us lasted for around twelve months and then, almost as suddenly as she had arrived, she returned to Galley Common to live with Uncle Joe and Aunt Mary again. Her health had continued to deteriorate and my mother didn't really have the time to devote extra attention to her as well as looking after Fiona and me. Going up the stairs to her (my) bedroom had become an increasing struggle for her and so it was agreed that Joe and Mary would provide Gran with a room on the ground floor of their house. They came to collect her one Sunday afternoon and that was the last time I was to see both Gran and them. With Gran's departure, I was finally able to return to my bedroom, this time permanently. It had been a long wait - I was now sixteen.

At school, things had begun to get a little more serious. I was now in the fourth form with the prospect of maths and English language 'O' level exams looming at the end of the school year. Maths was now taught by a new young master called Mr Howden, who had just arrived at our school. He was a decent teacher but rather short-tempered and very strict. He was called 'Flinty' by us boys due to his stern nature. For some inexplicable reason, in our very first lesson with him, he started to address me as Peach instead of Heather. There was no-one called Peach in my class or indeed in the whole school so it was strange that he used this name. The first time he did this was very confusing but I realized that as he was clearly looking at me, I must have been the boy he was trying to communicate with. I simply ignored his error and responded anyway. I reasoned that as he was new, he couldn't yet know everyone's name correctly. However, despite trying to politely correct his mistake each time, he continued to call me Peach. Other boys in class thought it was hilarious and a few even started calling me Peachy outside of the classroom. After a few weeks of this mistaken identity farce, when he once again called me Peach in his lesson, I stood up and forcibly told him that he was wrong. My correct name was Heather, I added and would he please remember that in future. For a moment or two there was complete silence in the room and you could have heard a pin drop. He stood staring at me from the front of the class and then something snapped. He strode towards me with his eyes glaring and said 'How dare you speak to me like that? Your name is Peach.' He emphasised the last four words by poking me in the chest with his forefinger. He paused for a moment and then slapped me hard across the face 'for being insolent.' I was stunned, mentally and physically and slowly sat down, close to tears. The teacher returned to the front of the shocked class and continued the lesson as if nothing had just happened.

As Mr Howden was also our class master and the normal avenue to address such an issue was therefore closed, I went to see the deputy head to complain about what had happened. Presumably, they must have discussed the matter with 'Flinty' because a couple of days later during a review of our homework in the next maths lesson, I was amazed when the teacher pointed at me and asked, 'What answer have you got, Heather?' The way he said my name was as if he had been using it correctly since the start of term. Nothing was ever said and there was no apology for his assault or confusion over my name but fortunately, I remained Heather for the rest of my time at school.

In complete contrast was my favourite teacher, our English master, a kindly old gentleman from Yorkshire called Mr Scott. I usually enjoyed his lessons though I'm sure he despaired at times of me ever learning the finer intricacies of English grammar and literature. However, his patience and encouragement over the ensuing years were an important factor in my developing a strong interest in our language and literature as well as a love of books in general. It's a pity he is no longer with us to see that all his patient efforts were not entirely wasted. I also enjoyed my art lessons. I was not particularly gifted at it but showed some talent in design and layout which I developed further in later life. Latin was my Achilles heel (or should that be the heel of Achilleus?) and I could never get the hang of my Latin primer. I probably spent too much time during the afternoon lessons gazing out of the classroom window while the Punic Wars went on all around me. I always felt that the Romans spent too much time trying to conquer the rest of the world and not enough on sorting out their declensions and syntax.

In 1959, I had my first taste of voting in an election. When, on the back of a strongly performing economy, the Conservative government called a general election for October that year, our headmaster decided to arrange for us boys to hold our own 'election'. Members of the Upper Sixth were allowed to stand for whichever party they chose, real or invented and on the actual election day, we were all 'enfranchised' and could cast our vote for whomever we wanted. The choice of parties was broad. As well as candidates for the Tories, Labour and Liberals, there was a Communist, Nationalist and a couple of Independents. In the week of the run-up to the election, there was great excitement in the school. Party manifestos were written and handed out, posters appeared on the walls and corridors and speeches made in the playground at break-time with predictable raucous booing and shouting from the schoolboy electorate. It was the most exciting week at school that I can remember. The result was announced by the Head during a noisy morning assembly the day after the real election. Perhaps unsurprisingly, the school Conservative candidate won by a healthy majority, mirroring the actual national result.[14] What was somewhat surprising was that the school's Communists were the runners-up, presumably due to the fact that their candidate was a boy who was very popular and respected in school. It just goes to show how a strong personality can sometimes triumph over weak policies in an election.

In the spring of 1960, I decided to try to find some kind of a job. I had left the choir more than a year ago when my voice finally broke, so that useful source of income had disappeared and I was feeling the absence of any pocket money. The obvious choice was a paper-round but when I asked at the nearby newsagents where Pat had worked, I was told there were no vacancies. It seems that not many people on our council estate took delivery of a daily newspaper. A few weeks later in the playground at break-time, I heard one of the fifth-formers asking around if anyone was interested in a job at a chemist shop in town. My ears instantly picked up and I asked him what was involved. He told me that it was an easy job, basically stocking up the shelves, working for an hour or so each weekday evening straight after school plus four hours on Saturday mornings. He was now giving up the job to concentrate on preparing for his 'O' level exams. It seemed straightforward enough and when he told me that the pay was ten shillings a week, I grabbed my opportunity and told him I would like to take over from him.

The boy's name was Ray Cox and a few days later after school, I went with him for an interview. The chemist shop was Hutton & Barratt on the corner of Warwick Street and The Parade. I had a short chat with the manager and the pharmacist in the dispensary and then Ray showed me around the stock rooms and explained more about the job. When we returned, the pharmacist told me the job was

---

[14] The Tories under Harold MacMillan increased their majority from 60 seats to 100.

mine and I could start the following Monday. I rushed home on my bike to let my mother know that I had finally found a job and would be paid ten shillings a week. I promised that I would keep a couple of shillings as pocket money and give the remainder to her as a small but important contribution to the household finances. It was nearly enough to pay for our weekly joint of New Zealand lamb which I collected from the butcher on Saturday afternoons.

As Ray had indicated, the job proved to be relatively easy. There was some heavy lifting, moving deliveries down to the stock room in the cellar and then carrying supplies back up to go on the shelves in the shop. The hardest part was accessing a separate storage area in the attic of a small, adjacent building where all the different sizes of medicine bottles, pill boxes etc. were kept. They were stored in rows of cardboard boxes set out on wooden racks. The ground floor was used as a garage by the manager who lived in a flat directly above the chemist shop. The only access to the attic was up a near vertical step ladder from the back of the garage. It required a considerable feat of balancing on my part to carry boxes of supplies up and down this ladder and then carefully manoeuvre around the manager's car. In the summer, it wasn't too bad but as I discovered once the cold, dark days of mid-winter arrived, it was both dangerous and a little scary. The problem was that there was no lighting in the garage or attic. I could prop open the door leading into the shop to provide some light into the garage but up in the attic, it was almost pitch black. I fumbled around in the dark, trying to locate the appropriate boxes containing the various items required in the dispensary. I hated walking into trailing cobwebs that caught on my face but the worst thing were the occasional birds that got in that would suddenly fly past me, wings flapping, when disturbed.

When I later asked Ray about it, he told me he initially kept a couple of candles up there but was soon banned from doing this due to the fire risk so he had used a torch. I didn't own a torch so I one Saturday morning I rearranged things so it was easier to memorize the locations of the most-used boxes. However, this only worked to a limited extent and I soon resorted to keeping a box of matches hidden in a corner at the entrance to the attic. There was usually just enough light from one or two flickering matches to do what I needed up there. I reasoned that as long as management didn't know about the matches, I would be OK and I was always most careful to collect the spent matchsticks after use. Despite the winter attic problems, I mostly enjoyed working there. The staff were pleasant and easy to talk to and I much appreciated the ten shillings each week. In the end, I stayed on for two years until, like Ray before me, it was my turn to prepare for 'O' level exams

After I had taken the job, Ray and I stayed in touch at school and one day that summer he mentioned to me that he was a member of an amateur rocket club. Not having previously met anyone from a rocket club, I was extremely impressed and asked what this involved. Ray explained that he and some friends, most of whom lived in London designed and built rockets, yes real rockets that they launched them from remote sites around the UK. He showed me a couple of photos of rockets that they had already built. Their current ambition was to beat the existing UK record for the highest altitude attained by an amateur-built rocket. At the time, the British Government's Blue Streak ballistic missile programme was in full swing and interest in rocketry and space exploration was high, both among professionals and amateurs.[15] This all sounded terribly exciting to me and so when Ray asked me if I was interested in helping, I instantly said yes.

---

[15] The launch of the Russian Sputnik in October 1957 greatly increased interest in rockets and space and the number of amateur groups like ours grew significantly in both the UK and around the world. The UK Rocketry Association was eventually formed in 1996.

Over the next few weeks I went around to Ray's house several times where he talked me through in detail what they had previously done and showed me some of the parts he was making for their next project. We also met with two other enthusiasts who drove over from Coventry - John who was around eighteen or nineteen years old and Graham who was in his early twenties. Ray and the other two were clearly very knowledgeable about chemistry and mechanics and the couple of rockets they had previously launched looked very impressive to me. In complete contrast, I was a total novice when it came to that kind of technical knowledge. Despite this, the other three assured me that I would be of use in helping to assemble components and especially when it came to launching the rocket later in the year.

Their design for the attempt on the British record was a two-stage rocket and we in Leamington were responsible for the top or final stage. The lower section was being built by other members of the group in London. Progress was quite rapid and by the end of the summer term, both sections had been constructed and a launch date in August during the summer holidays was set. The plan was for the four of us from Leamington to drive down to London in Graham's car to link up with the others. The whole group would then drive over to mid-Wales where we would camp for a couple of days while the launch took place. So it was, that one Friday morning a couple of weeks later, we set off in Graham's Morris Minor, arriving several hours later at a house in Hounslow. This was where Mike, the overall leader of the group, lived. It was a rather ordinary 1930s semi-detached house and somehow was not what I had expected as the headquarters of a potentially record-breaking rocketry group. Similarly, Mike was not at all the boffin-like person I had anticipated. He turned out to be a pleasant, easy-going, slightly chubby but quite ordinary married man in his mid-thirties. Shortly after our arrival, we were joined by one of the other experts from London who was to travel with us on the trip to Wales. He was about the same age as Mike but tall and gangly with a ragged beard and was called the 'Prof' or professor. As far as I was concerned, here was someone whose nickname and appearance at last fitted with the image I had in my mind for a group of mad rocket scientists. We spent the evening making sure that the various sections of the rocket all fitted together and the controls functioned properly before settling down for the night in sleeping bags on Mike's living room floor.

After a hearty breakfast of fried eggs, baked beans and toast, we loaded up Mike's van with all the rocket components, materials for the fuel mix and launch plus our food and a couple of tents. We then set off for Wales – the Leamington group in Graham's car and Mike and the 'Prof' in the van. The M4 motorway was not even a dream in a planner's mind so the journey westwards was long and slow. We eventually arrived in the late afternoon at some desolate spot with a seemingly unpronounceable name in central Wales on the northern edge of the Black Mountains. As we off-loaded the vehicles and set up out tents in a field, Mike explained to me that it was very difficult to get permission to launch our type of rocket. A very large open space with no buildings, people, roads or overhead wires was required. One of Mike's relations knew the local landowner who had given his permission for our launch. Well, the spot chosen by Mike was certainly remote and it was bleak, very bleak. It was also raining hard, quite windy and misty. I couldn't see any sign of human existence apart from the nearby farm track by which we had arrived and a few sheep in a distant field. All around us lay soggy green fields and rugged, cloud-topped hills. Perfect territory apparently for a good rocket launch but not so pleasant if you are trying to erect a tent on a muddy slope.

By the time we got the tents up and a brew going, the weather had improved and the rain more or less stopped. After a makeshift dinner cooked on a camper stove, we all turned in for an early night, ready for the excitement of the following day. The next morning, following the now traditional rocket man's breakfast of baked beans and eggs (but no toast), we loaded up all our equipment and set off deeper into the Welsh countryside. After half a mile or so of walking, Mike pronounced that this was our launch site and we then spent a couple of hours carefully setting all the gear. Once fully assembled, our rocket was about seven feet tall and looked very impressive as its steel casing sections caught the weak morning sun's rays. I helped Ray carefully lift it into a vertical position, balanced on its four fins. After a few last-minute checks, Mike eventually declared everything was ready and it was a '*go for launch.*' We all retreated into a small dip around a hundred yards away from the rocket and the countdown began. At the shout of '*zero*', the Prof pushed the button on his control unit that was wired up to our rocket. A fraction of a second later, there was a bright flash and a burning whoosh as the rocket tried to escape from earth's gravity and climb up towards the hazy blue sky. It rose perhaps fifty feet before a sudden, loud explosion in the lower section caused the whole rocket to initially veer off to the right and then tumble back down to earth with a devastating crunch.

The disbelief and disappointment were clear on everyone's face. How could this have happened, what went wrong? Our combined dreams of beating the British record now lay in shattered pieces on the soggy Welsh field in front of us. My brief excitement had lasted less than a minute – it was all over too quickly. I readily admit that I didn't really understand the subsequent technical discussions at the debrief, though I seem to remember the problem was deemed to be something to do with the fuel mixture. I have to say that my fellow rocketeers were very stoical about the whole thing – for them it wasn't the first time such an event had occurred. As with anyone else at the cutting edge of science, it was back to the drawing board and try again.

As the day was still young, Mike suggested that there was time for a short diversion on the way home to visit some nearby, interesting old abandoned gold mines that he knew of. With nothing else to do, we all agreed and set off for the mines which lay a few miles north. Mike explained that he had visited this area a couple of years ago while on holiday and had found an entrance into one of the mine galleries and was sure he could locate it again. He told us that the mines originated from Roman times but although they were now worked out and derelict, who knew what we might find.[16] True to his word, Mike eventually found the right spot. After walking along a little-used path and pushing past some brambles and nettles, we saw a rocky outcrop with a small tunnel entrance in front of us. Prof had a torch and we filed into the mine entrance after him, gradually descending the cool, dark mine drift. It was an eerie experience inside with the only sounds being our footsteps and water droplets falling from the roof. As we went further in, the silence was suddenly broken when someone shouted out 'gold!' We all pushed forward and gathered around an area of wall where in the torchlight, we could see that there were a few glittering golden specks. Could these really be nuggets of gold? No-one was sure but we instantly broke into a frenzy of excited activity and using our pocket knives, we each managed to prise loose a thumb-sized nugget of dark grey rock containing traces of sparkling material. After that, we explored the dark tunnel a little longer until we could go no further due to a rock-fall. It was time to leave anyway, so we turned around and headed back out to the cars for the long journey home.

When Graham dropped me off at home late that evening, I rushed in to tell my mother about all my adventures and proudly produced the small nugget of rock from my pocket to show her. She inspected it briefly and then told me it was almost certainly 'fool's gold' and not

---

[16] I believe these were the Dolaucothi gold mines, Roman surface and underground mines on what is now National Trust land in the River Cothi valley, Carmarthenshire.

real. My intense disappointment can be imagined but undeterred, I kept my little piece of Welsh rock for many years in a small box in a cupboard. It was an interesting souvenir of a fun but ultimately foolish weekend in Wales. Some weeks after our return, I decided that rocketry was not for me and I let Ray know. He told me he would continue to build rockets but as he left school that year, I lost touch with him and have no idea of whether he ever had any rocketing success.

Chapter Five
A REVEALING EXPERIENCE

My short adventure in Wales was the only holiday or time away from home I had while we lived in Lillington until I reached the age of seventeen. By then, I managed to save up enough money from various jobs to help pay for a one-week school sixth-form skiing holiday, travelling by train to France. As before in Kenilworth Road, we couldn't afford to go away on holiday due to our financial situation. But now, even the occasional day trip by coach that we had previously enjoyed was impractical as it was simply too difficult with Fiona (and later my Gran) to reach the coach station which lay at far end of town. We never went to the cinema or theatre in Leamington and the only time I can recall us going out as a family was when we went to church on Sunday evenings.

Although I was never particularly bored during the school holidays, I did spend a lot of time by myself, either playing in the house or messing around in the garden when the weather was fine. I still cycled around town delivering my mother's dressmaking output and of course, I now had my job at the chemist's shop. However, with time on my hands and the desire to earn more pocket money, I increasingly sought job opportunities during the holidays. For several months in early 1961, I had been watching a gang of builders at work on the empty adjacent plot around the corner in Valley Road. They were constructing a terrace of three homes identical to the one in which we lived in Wellington Road[17]. The week before the school

---

[17] Although I didn't know it at the time, I was actually helping to build our future home. In 1966, our house in Wellington Road had severe structural problems so we were moved by the council into the equivalent middle house in this Valley Road terrace.

Easter holidays, I decided to go around to see the foreman and ask whether there was any chance of working as a labourer on site during my holiday. The foreman was quite happy to take me on as they were running behind schedule. I spent most of the time working for one of the bricklayers, off-loading bricks and cement from the delivery wagons and then carrying them up the scaffolding in a hod. But one day, something entirely different happened. The delivery wagon didn't show up and as we had virtually run out of bricks, the foreman decided that he and I would go in his van to collect some from the builder's merchants in Warwick. As we drove along, the foreman explained that they quite often ran out of supplies and he regularly had to drive over to Warwick. When we pulled into the large builders' yard a little later, he turned to me and with a conspiratorial wink said, 'You're going to enjoy this.' I had no idea what he meant but I was in fact already enjoying the rest from my labouring duties. After filling out some paperwork, we went into the warehouse and the foreman shouted to one of the men inside 'Is Maria around today? I've got a young man here who'd like to see her!'

'Yes, she's over at the back of the timber section' came the reply. As the foreman duly led the way to the timber section, I asked who Maria was and why he was taking me to meet her. 'You'll see' was his only response.

We worked our way to the back of the warehouse and as we rounded a stack of pallets, we almost bumped into a pretty, young blonde woman, about the same age as me. The foreman greeted her like an old friend and then introduced us, 'Maria, this is Rod and Rod, this is Tits.' For a second, I thought I had misheard but when the foreman bluntly said 'C'mon, show us your tits' I knew that I hadn't. Maria or Tits was clearly a little coy at first and said she didn't want to show them to me as she didn't know me. But after a bit more encouragement from the foreman, she suddenly grabbed the bottom of her sweater with both hands and yanked it up to her face. My eyes nearly sprang from their sockets. Before me, not more than a couple of feet away, were the most gorgeous pair of perfectly-formed, bra-less female breasts I had ever seen. I can confidently say they were perfect as up to that point, I had never actually seen a woman's real breasts, except in photographs. I was both mildly embarrassed and stunned into silence and didn't know what to say or do. My young life so far had not prepared me for this momentous occasion; what does one say to a pretty, young woman who has just willingly revealed to you her fine breasts? 'Do you want to feel them?' she suddenly asked as she jiggled them around temptingly in front of me. But before I could reach out and touch them, she pulled the front of her sweater back down and said teasingly, 'That's enough for now' before wandering off further into the warehouse, her breasts gently jiggling in time to the rhythm of her seductive gait.

I stood motionless, staring lustily after the retreating blonde until the foreman dragged me away back out into the yard. 'Thought you'd enjoy that' he said. 'She appears shy but actually she likes turning the men on by flashing her tits' he continued. Well, I was certainly turned on and couldn't even remember subsequently returning to the arduous job of loading the bricks into the van. Now I understood why the foreman was happy to regularly drive to the builders' merchant to collect the bricks. That night, as I lay in bed thinking about Maria, I briefly considered whether I should skip school for a few weeks and stay on at the building site in the hope of seeing 'Tits' again. It clearly wasn't a sensible plan but I could see at least two significant and very attractive benefits. However, sense prevailed and I never saw her again.

When we had started back at school in the fourth form the previous September, we were all given the option of either continuing to play rugby as a winter sport or taking up hockey. I never particularly enjoyed my school rugger. It seemed a very stop-start sport and grovelling around in a muddy field on a cold winter's day was not my idea of fun.

So, I chose hockey and played each Wednesday afternoon through the autumn and winter terms. I soon found that I not only enjoyed the game but also had an aptitude for it. Within a couple of months, I not only started playing for the school team but the following summer I was also selected for a junior county trial which would give me the chance of playing for Warwickshire in the autumn. This was all very encouraging but when I entered the fifth form in September 1960, I increasingly found that my job at the chemist interfered with my hockey ambitions. The first problem was that there were regular weekly team practice sessions arranged by the hockey master after school which I couldn't attend due to my job. Initially, this wasn't too serious and I got by with a variety of excuses for not participating. However, once competitive school matches started which were played on Saturday mornings, my non-availability for the team became a major issue. I finally had to admit that I had a job and wouldn't be able to play in the team at all that year. The hockey master berated me for letting both the team and school down. He then reported me to the headmaster who called me to his office one morning to discuss the matter. I tried to explain how important the job was financially, both to me and my mother but I don't think the headmaster was totally convinced by my explanation. He then wrote to my mother expressing disappointment at the situation and asking that we reconsider whether it was appropriate for me to be working, especially in a job that took up so much time.

In a way, he was right. I was already finding it difficult to cope with the increased amount of homework in the fifth form and of course, I missed playing for the school team. I discussed the situation with my mother and although she said it was my choice, I knew we would miss the money and I would once again have no pocket money. I informed the hockey master the next morning that I felt unable to give up my job and therefore would not be able to play for the team. A few days later during the morning assembly, the headmaster in his address talked about how boys in the fifth and sixth forms should avoid taking jobs and concentrate on their important school work. After that, I was definitely on the headmaster's 'watch list' and felt as if I had been blackballed at school. Unfortunately, the whole episode got under my skin; I was annoyed with the school and frustrated with my situation. I became disinterested in lessons and put little effort into my work, with the end-result being that I did poorly in my 'O' level exams the following summer.

A few weeks before I was due to sit my 'O' levels in the late spring of 1961, my father visited us in Lillington. He had stayed in touch over the years, periodically sending letters and photos, either of him driving his latest car or on holiday which was usually somewhere in Florida. I was happy to receive the letters and see the photos but I know it irked my mother. On one occasion when I showed her the latest photo of my father sitting in a smart-looking convertible alongside a beach. She glanced at it said 'It's all very fine for your father. We could do with a holiday.' It was one of the very rare occasions that my mother ever referred negatively to our situation or my father in this way.

My father was now on his way back to Canada from the Far East where he had been working as an air traffic control adviser for the ICAO[18] for the previous two years. I was happy to see him again and I think my mother was too. He was with us for a long weekend, staying once again at a hotel in Leamington and as on his previous visit, he rented a car. We spent the weekend happily driving around, visiting some of his old war-time haunts including his former RAF base at Gaydon, a few miles south of Leamington. Although still operational, it had inevitably changed substantially since my father's flying days there and I remember he was most upset to see a line of washing strung out from the remnants of the old control tower. We also went over to Coventry to see the haunting ruins of the

---

[18] ICAO – International Civil Aviation Organization, based in Montreal, the ICAO is an agency of the United Nations.

city's cathedral that been bombed by the Germans during the War. On the way home, we stopped in Kenilworth and had lunch in a pub opposite the castle. My father ordered a pint of draught English bitter which was 'warm', just as he remembered it from the War. He was glad to see that some things hadn't changed in England. By the time that I entered the fifth form, I was really starting to shoot up in height. Until then at grammar school, I had been only average height. Now, as we now stood side by side in the Kenilworth pub, my father was surprised to see that I was slightly taller than him. My head just reached one of the old oak beams that supported the ceiling whereas his head didn't quite reach it.

That evening, my father and mother went out together in the car to Leamington for dinner. It was good to see my mother dressed up for an evening out and with a hint of a sparkle in her eyes. It was dusk when I heard the car pull up outside our house and when I briefly looked out of the window, I could just make out that there was a bit of romancing going on in the car. I left them to it and when my mother came in a while later, she was missing an earring and her hair which she usually wore in a bun, was slightly undone. She didn't say anything to me but it was clear she had enjoyed her evening out and I was happy for her. My father was leaving the next morning and he came to the house to say goodbye to us. He gave me a couple of presents that he had bought in the Far East, a soap stone chess set and a camera with two rolls of film. I had taken up chess a few years earlier at school (I actually played in the team a few times) and so appreciated the chess set. I also appreciated the camera but as I subsequently found, I could rarely afford to buy more film and pay for the development and printing of my photos.

It was sad to see my father leave once more to return to Canada but I was heartened by the apparent affection I had witnessed between my parents. My optimism was reinforced when my mother told me later about the discussion they had over dinner the previous evening. My father had asked if they could get back together and my mother had promised that she would give the idea serious consideration. However, a few weeks later, my mother told me that she had now written to my father to say that she had decided that it wouldn't work and we would continue as we were in Lillington. She went on to say that it was now certain that they would divorce. I never knew the exact details of what the two of them had discussed or the potential arrangements for getting back together but it was clear from what my mother said that Fiona's future remained an important stumbling block. I was extremely disappointed and upset, as I know my mother was too. It was a difficult decision for her to take and it wasn't done lightly but the future and its impact on my parents, Fiona and I was now cast for better or for worse.

Sure enough, within a few months, their divorce was finalised. It seemed strange to me that such an important matter could be settled in such a relatively short time. I had always harboured a tiny hope that somehow my parents would eventually re-unite and we would be together as a family, either in England or Canada. So, when my mother told me the news, it was an extremely sad moment and I remember how we wept together in each other's arms. The only small ray of sunlight at that otherwise very dark time, was the fact that my mother received a small cash settlement from my father of one thousand pounds. My mother showed me the banker's draft that had arrived a little while after the divorce papers. To me at the time, it seemed an enormous sum of money, almost beyond anything I could comprehend. And indeed, it soon provided a significant change in our general living standards as well as somewhat easing the burden on my mother financially. But the reality was that although the money now gave us a financial safety net or cushion, it proved to be nowhere near enough to alter our situation and allow my mother to stop working.

The first concrete evidence as far as I was concerned of our improved finances was the wrist watch my mother bought me for my sixteenth birthday that September. It was my first watch and made me realise how relatively unimportant knowledge of the exact time had been in my life so far. Not having a watch had generally not been a problem for me. The only time-piece in our home was a battered old wind-up alarm clock in mother's bedroom which pierced the morning silence to get us up each day. Otherwise, our life at home was regulated by the TV or radio. At school, the routine rhythms of the classroom controlled my life and along with 650 other boys, I responded to the hourly ringing of the school bell. My first watch was something of a bitter-sweet occasion as it brought to mind the unfortunate sequence of events when I had borrowed my cousin Brian's watch some years before.

My mother was also able to buy me a much-needed new black blazer for the sixth form and other material acquisitions soon followed. First, we acquired a telephone which was a significant help to my mother in arranging appointments with her clients and then a couple of months later, we finally bought a car. This was a second-hand, pale blue Isetta bubble car which was made by BMW in Germany. The Isetta was small (only 7.5 feet long by 4.5 feet wide) and egg-shaped, with a single bench seat and a small parcel shelf behind over the rear-mounted engine. There were two wheels at each front corner and a pair of closely-spaced small tandem wheels at the rear. The entire front of the car which contained a large windscreen, hinged outwards to allow entry. In the event of a crash, the driver was supposed to exit through the folding canvas sunroof. The steering wheel and small instrument binnacle swung out with the single door, making access to the bench seat quite easy. The car was essentially designed for two people though my mother, Fiona and I were just able to squeeze in alongside each other.

The little Isetta was powered by a 236 cc two-stroke motorcycle engine producing just 9.5 horsepower and driven through a notchy manual gearbox with four forward speeds and reverse. Our newly-acquired bubble car needed around thirty seconds to reach 30mph and its top speed was less than 50mph. It was a very different type of vehicle from the expensive executive cars that BMW manufacture today. Keeping up with other traffic or maintaining progress up steep hills was sometimes problematic, especially if all three of us were on board but that rarely diminished our fun. Despite its obvious limitations, it was an ideal starter car for us; parking was a joy and its excellent fuel economy (it could achieve anywhere from 50-70mpg depending on how it was driven) meant our running costs were low. My mother had learnt to drive when we lived in Canada but her licence was invalid for the UK and so she had to take driving lessons and eventually managed to pass her test on the second attempt. Along with thousands of other families across the country, the acquisition of our first car provided us with a new-found freedom. We could now enjoy days out in the countryside, pop into Leamington for shopping and for my mother, visiting her clients was infinitely easier than on her old bike. Once I learned to drive a little later, it gave me greater independence and a much-improved social life. We kept the little Isetta for about two years; it served us well, proved generally reliable and used very little petrol.

There was one other important thing that occurred while I was in the fifth year at school. The government announced the end of National Service or conscription into the armed forces which had been in place since the Second World War. All healthy males between the ages of seventeen and twenty-one were expected to serve for two years and then remain on the reserve list for three years. Despite the fact that the system had gradually been winding down since 1957, call-ups were only formally ended on 31 December 1960. Although students were exempt, the likelihood of having to do National Service once our studies were finished hung over us like the sword of Damocles. The ending of National Service was regarded as such an important event that it was actually announced to the school during morning assembly. For me, the removal of the threat of having to do National Service meant that my desire to enter the sixth form and hopefully go on to university, was now much more feasible.

Despite the good news about National Service, as I waited for my 'O' level results to be announced that summer, it was by no means certain whether I would be able to go on into the sixth form or have to leave school at sixteen. Although our financial circumstances were now improved, my mother wasn't sure whether she could continue to support me for the next two years of sixth form. Even if I went into the sixth form, given my unimpressive academic record, there was no guarantee that I would obtain a university place and even if I did, it meant possibly a further three years of partial support by my mother. We discussed the problem on several occasions and although I desperately wanted to continue in education and prove myself, I had to respect my mother's feelings. We talked about various career possibilities during the early summer but nothing really seemed to stand out. Then, a couple of weeks before the 'O' level results came out, I noticed an advert for the Hong Kong Police Force. They were seeking seventeen to eighteen-year-old males to join the Force as cadets in Hong Kong. The exotic glamour of the colony and the Far East in general had an immediate appeal to me. The excited images in my mind were fuelled by the various colourful post cards of the region that I had received from Brian and my father over the past few years. Since I would reach the age of seventeen that September, I quickly sent off for an application form which arrived in the mail a few days later, together with an information pack about the Force's work.

Over the next couple of days, I carefully went through all the paperwork and discussed it with my mother. She understood why I was attracted to the position but there was clearly a hesitancy in her comments – I think she was understandably reluctant to see me follow in Brian's footsteps and disappear off to the far, Far East, probably for several years. In the end, she suggested that I should discuss the situation with our friend, Dr Elgood who might be able to advise me better. I went to see him a few days later and we went through the pros and cons of me going to Hong Kong. He was very understanding regarding the dilemma I faced but also very firm in encouraging me to wait for my results and to stay on at school as the best long term option. I decided to follow his advice and abandoned the idea of a career in the Hong Kong police force.

Shortly afterwards, I went into school one morning, along with the rest of the fifth-formers to receive our 'O' level results. The news was not good. I had only passed five 'O' levels, albeit with reasonable grades. I went home and told my mother about my mediocre achievement, expecting her to confirm that I should now find a job. It seems however, that unknown to me, Dr Elgood had also spoken to my mother and advised her that I really ought to stay on at school. So, to my surprise the words that I heard that morning from my mother were to the effect that I could have done better and must work harder if I could get into the sixth form. I rushed back to school and after a meeting with the headmaster, it was agreed that my results were just enough to allow me into the sixth form. I was very lucky.

Chapter Six
CARS, GIRLS AND DRUMS

From four classes in the 5th form with around thirty boys in each, we were now split into two Lower Sixth classes with some twenty pupils in each – one for science subjects and one for arts. I was in the latter, having chosen to study English literature, French and Geography at 'A' level. In addition, all of us sixth formers did 'A' level General Studies. The numbers choosing to enter the sixth form show that even for a grammar school in the early sixties, the student drop-out rate at this stage of their education was surprisingly high. Pupils were allowed to leave school at the age of fifteen then – the leaving age wasn't raised to sixteen until 1972. In addition, several boys also then left school at the end of Lower Sixth and of course, not everyone who stayed on obtained places at a university. I felt truly fortunate to have made it into the Sixth Form and although she never said as much, I think my mother was too.

Now that I had turned seventeen, I was keen to learn to drive. After some pleading, my mother agreed to pay for six lessons for me as my birthday present but she warned me that I had better learn fast as we couldn't afford any more. I duly took my test at the end of September and sadly, failed. Six lessons just weren't enough with no other driving practice. Undeterred, I raided my meagre savings and paid for two more lessons myself and on the day of my second test, I backed these up with a couple of hours driving around in an old A30 van that belonged to the father of one of my friends. This time I was successful and I was the first to pass the driving test in my year at school. For once in my life, I found myself ahead of my peer group with a much greater level of independence by now being able to drive. As I was increasingly allowed to use the car at weekends to go out with my friends, my social life improved significantly.

Some six months later, our love affair with the Isetta bubble burst in a rather abrupt way when my mother drove us to visit some friends of hers in Leamington one Sunday afternoon. When we pulled up outside their house and swung open the car's front door to get out, the steering wheel failed to move outwards with the door as normal and simply flopped down into my mother's lap. As we subsequently discovered, the retaining bolts attaching the steering wheel to the door had sheered, totally without warning. Had this happened while we were driving along the road, it could have been fatal. Although it was quickly and easily repaired at the garage in Lillington, my mother understandably lost faith in the little Isetta. It was soon replaced with a more expensive but much more usable and stylish two-year-old, white Morris Minor convertible.

With a more active social life and the resultant cost of buying petrol for the car, my lack of money eventually drove me to look for another job. By pure chance, I bumped into one of the girls who worked in the chemist shop with me earlier. She was still there and told me that they had another branch near the top of The Parade that was currently looking for someone to work there every Saturday. I called in to the shop the next day and met with the pharmacist. The job was very similar to the one I had done previously except that their supplies were stored in the cellar, not in an unlit attic and I was expected to help out a bit in the dispensary. The pay rate for the Saturday was the same ten shillings as at the other branch which was fine by me. Once I had told him about my previous experience, he immediately offered me the job and I started the following Saturday.

As I soon learnt, things in this chemist were quite different from the previous one. Although technically under the overall control of the same manager who lived above the other Hutton and Barratt's, the pharmacist at my new place of work was effectively left to run things by himself. I recognize that I am misusing the word 'effectively' here because my new boss was extremely disorganised. The dispensary which was behind a large screen at the back of the shop and therefore fortunately out of sight of our customers, was invariably a complete mess when I arrived each Saturday morning. Paperwork would be chaotically strewn around, dispensing bottles and pill boxes left out on the counter and because he was a heavy smoker, at least one lit cigarette would be smouldering somewhere in the dispensary. He also liked a drink and was an inveterate gambler on the horses. In addition, he was a Scot and tended to mumble brusquely in a gruff accent that was often hard to understand, especially if he had been drinking. The place was a world away from the tidy, well-run chemist that I had previously worked in.

My first task each Saturday morning was to clear up the mess and try to bring some order to the dispensary, only then could I get on with my proper work. Although it was difficult at first trying to adjust to the vagaries of my new boss, we soon developed a reasonable working relationship. Once I had shown that I could do the job, he started to trust me and ask me to do more. I placed orders for stock if he was busy, helped him prepare simple prescriptions and answered the phone when he was out. I soon discovered that the main reasons for his regular absences from the shop were either to go and buy a bottle of whisky or to visit the nearby bookmaker. If he was exceptionally busy or thought the manager might be calling in, he would occasionally ask me to go along to the bookie to place his bets – something that I did not particularly enjoy, even if it got me out of the shop for a while. Overall though, I was happy there and must have done a decent job as he would sometimes ask me to work additional days during my school holidays. I remained at the chemist until a month or so before my 'A' level exams.

After school, especially on Friday afternoons, the favourite place to go for many of Leamington's sixth formers (boys and girls) was an Italian coffee bar half way along the south side of Regent Street. It was the one spot in town in which to both meet friends and to be seen. It was called Franco's and was actually owned and run by an Italian family. Over cappuccinos in small glass cups, with the latest hit singles playing on the juke box, all the latest teenage gossip was exchanged in an increasingly lively atmosphere. Plans for the weekend were explored, rumours of any parties eagerly seized on and occasionally, new romances blossomed. As I didn't get paid until Saturday for my job in the chemist shop, I rarely had money for a coffee on Fridays. I was not the only one facing this predicament and we were known as the NDs – no drinks. The lugubrious but eagle-eyed Italian waiter constantly circled the coffee bar trying to catch anyone sitting at a table without a drink and so we developed the ND game. The rules were simple. If you were an ND, you tried to ensure you sat with a large group, preferably in the middle in the hope that you wouldn't immediately be noticed and asked to order. If someone left, you grabbed their empty coffee cup and placed it in front of you. If the waiter approached before someone left, the group would shuffle the cups around on the table so that it wasn't easy to see whether everyone had a drink. If you were lucky and practised at the game, it was often possible for the NDs to stretch out our time in the coffee bar for half an hour or more. However, the important, golden rule was that once eventually caught by the waiter, you left immediately in order to prevent any fuss or embarrassment to the rest of the group.

The music we youngsters listened to on the café juke box or at home in the early sixties was a bit of an odd mixture. The Hit Parade at that time contained an evolving, eclectic range of artistes. The established stars of the late 1950s such as Perry Como, Bobby Darin and Connie Francis were steadily being replaced by a younger, more raucous wave of new American singers such as Elvis Presley, The Everly Brothers, Neil Sedaka, Ricky Nelson,

Del Shannon and Buddy Holly. They in turn were competing with the growing number of home-grown talents like Cliff Richard, Tommy Steele, Adam Faith, Billy Fury and Helen Shapiro. While Chubby Checker was still twisting away, The Beatles and The Stones were yet to take centre stage on the British music scene. At home, Radio Luxembourg, with DJs like Pete Murray and Alan Freeman, remained the station to listen to, especially later at night. But in 1964, Radio Caroline, the first pirate radio station was launched and this gradually replaced Radio Luxembourg – at least for those who could receive the signal.

Sadly, the two good class-mates that I had in the lower school – the ones I had shared birthday parties with – did not go into the sixth form so once again, I was forced to make new friends. It took a while but eventually I became good friends with three boys in my new sixth form class – Mark Ryan, Colin Edwards and Frank Riley. It was Frank who was responsible for the introduction that brought about my first serious relationship with a member of the opposite sex. Frank, who lived close to Victoria Park on the far side of town had an older sister and her French penfriend, Claudine, came over on an exchange visit in the summer of 1962. She was seventeen and from St Nazaire in Brittany where her father was a senior manager of a large oil refinery. As both Frank and I were studying French 'A' level, Claudine's presence was an ideal opportunity to meet someone from France and try to improve our French language conversation skills. During the month she was in England, Claudine, Frank, his sister and I spent a lot of time together and I increasingly found that I really liked Claudine. She was lively, easy to get on with, enjoyed sports and playing games, especially cards and her charming French accent when speaking English simply added to her appeal. It was also evident to me that Claudine enjoyed my company. As we sat talking in Frank's house on the day before her return to France, somehow the subject of plans for next summer came up and I asked Claudine whether she would like to return to

Leamington next year by doing an exchange with me. It was a spur of the moment invitation; I hadn't thought through where would she sleep in our small house or how our respective parents would react to doing such an exchange or indeed how I would raise the funds to travel to France. Claudine looked at me for a few moments, no doubt a little surprised at the unexpected invitation and then with a flutter of her brown eyes, she said, 'Yes, yes, I would like that very much but I must talk with my parents.'

Within a week, I had a letter from her to say that her parents had agreed to the arrangement and she was looking forward to seeing me again next summer. Although at the time, I was happy with her positive response, a year was a long time away and I wasn't sure if she would really come. However, we continued to write regularly to each other and in July 1963, Claudine flew into Heathrow and then came up by train to Leamington. The twelve months' interval gave me time to both discuss arrangements with my mother and to start saving some money for my holiday. I could tell that my mother was in two minds about the visit. In one way, she was both pleased and intrigued that a young French woman would be staying in our home for a month. After all, she spoke a little French herself and had always encouraged me in my attempts to learn the language. On the other hand, she was concerned about not having any free time to entertain Claudine, our finances (another person to feed and my travel costs) and how this young Frenchwoman would react to staying in our small council house. Claudine was clearly from a relatively well-off family and my mother thought she might find our living arrangements a bit basic. In the end, I managed to allay most of her worries. We agreed that Claudine would have my bedroom and I would sleep on Brian's old bed in my mother's work-room. I promised I would find the money to contribute extra to the housekeeping while Claudine was with us as well as to pay for my visit to France.

Of course, the latter was more easily said than done. Along with a few of my friends, I was fortunate to get a job for a couple of weeks in December with the Post Office to help with the Christmas mail rush. Although I saved most of the money I earned, it was less than I needed, especially as I subsequently stopped working at the chemist in May in order to concentrate on my 'A' levels. However, once the exams were over, I had a few weeks before Claudine arrived and was lucky to find a couple of short-term jobs. I worked as a labourer on a building site in town and then as a waiter at the Royal Agricultural Show in Stoneleigh. Although I now had enough money to give my mother some extra cash for housekeeping and to cover day-to-day holiday expenses in both England and France, I realised I still didn't have quite enough to pay for my flights. So, I reluctantly sold the Grundig tape recorder that I had saved up for and bought last year and with that money, I now had just enough to cover everything.

Claudine arrived in early July 1963 and our relationship immediately resumed from where we had left it last summer. She was a delight to be with, full of good fun and humour and her French charm even won over my mother. With her long, auburn hair and short summer dresses that showed off her tanned, slim figure, she drew admiring glances wherever we went. I was, however, surprised to discover that she didn't shave her armpits but love conquers all, even hairy armpits. We spent all day, every day together and unsurprisingly, we became very intimate with each other, emotionally and physically. Claudine was the first female of my own age with whom I had spent any time or held any prolonged conversations and I was totally infatuated with her. Inevitably, my mother caught us kissing and cuddling on the couch in our front room a couple of times which did not go down well. She must have known and understood what was happening but evidently found it hard to accept that she had a teenage son, full of hormones. I borrowed my mother's car to show

Claudine the sights around Leamington and we also spent time going out with Frank and his sister or at their house. The month seemed to fly by and all too soon it was time to leave for France. We took the train from Leamington to London and then the bus out to Heathrow for the short Air France flight to St. Nazaire. It was my first experience of flying and like most first-timers, I was fascinated by the view through the window of the fluffy, white clouds and the green fields below stretching away to the horizon.

Claudine and her family lived in a spacious apartment in St Nazaire where we stayed the first two nights. However, the rest of my stay in France was spent in the nearby resort of La Baule where they had rented a holiday cottage right on sea front. It was a great location in which to spend the month of August. The weather was generally fine and sunny, the beach and sea were on our doorstep and there were lots of things to do in the town itself. A couple of Claudine's close friends from St Nazaire were also staying in La Baule that month and so the pair of us spent a lot of time with them. One of the boys had an old, rag-top Fiat 500 and four or five of us would somehow cram into it and zoom off along the Brittany coast to spend the day exploring and having fun. Although my romance with Claudine in La Baule initially continued as before, it became less intimate and our ardour gradually cooled. Surrounded by her friends most of the day and under the watchful eye of her parents in the evenings, we had little private time together. It was frustrating for both of us but there was nothing we could do about it.

My stay in France brought several new experiences – both good and bad. Forced to speak French every day, I found that both my vocabulary and fluency increased in leaps and bounds. I loved the fact that I could help myself anytime to a bottle of *Coca-Cola* from the fridge – it was a pleasure that I rarely enjoyed at home. I also generally enjoyed the French food that Claudine's mother prepared but didn't care for the fresh 'bigorneaux' and 'moules' (winkles and mussels) that we had a couple of times each week. Claudine and her parents liked to wander out to the rock pools in front of our house at low tide and collect these little 'delicacies' for us all to eat. Naturally, I was obliged to join in this harvesting process, but I was an unwilling participant. My stomach churned at the thought that an hour or so later, I would be confronted by a steaming plate piled high with these sea-creatures and expected to eat them all with a smile. I should add that later in life, with a more sophisticated palate, I learnt to enjoy mussels but I have never taken to winkles.

The other new experience that I still clearly remember was playing the drums in a group in a contest in the La Baule town hall. Claudine's friend who drove the old Fiat was the son of the sous-prefect[19] for the region. His name was Bruno and he lived with his parents in an imposing house in the best part of town. Soon after I had arrived, Claudine and I were invited to the house one evening to join Bruno and a few other teenagers for a small, casual party which was held in the large basement of the house. Bruno and three friends had recently formed an amateur pop group and I noticed their guitars and a full set of drums stacked in one corner of the basement. For some reason, I really wanted to have a go on the drums and eventually I asked Bruno if I could try. He willingly gave me a pair of drumsticks and I soon picked up the basics and ended up spending the rest of the night happily messing about on the drums. I really enjoyed myself, the more so as Claudine and Bruno said that I must have a natural talent for the drums.

Some two weeks later, Bruno turned up at our cottage one morning. He then explained to Claudine and me that his band had entered a talent competition at the town hall the following weekend and his drummer was ill in hospital. He wondered if I could possibly take his place? I was taken aback by this invitation. Messing about on the drums for an evening was one thing; playing the drums in

---

[19] A senior French government regional official

a band to proper music in a contest was something entirely different. Bruno sensed my reluctance and tried to encourage me by saying they were only playing two songs and there was plenty of time to practice over the next few days at his house. I looked at Claudine for guidance. Laughing, she took my arm and told me I should do it – she had every confidence in me and besides, it would be fun. I reluctantly gave in and agreed.

The four of us duly practiced several times and I eventually managed to get the rhythms and beats more or less right to accompany the guitar playing. However, I was still extremely nervous about the whole thing and when we arrived at the town hall on the Saturday night for the contest, I was staggered to see there were hundreds of people in the audience. Of the dozen or so acts that were performing that night, I was glad that we were second on the list. At least that meant my ordeal would be over quickly. We waited anxiously in the wings until it was our turn to perform and then walked out onto the stage. As I sat on my stool behind the drums, my legs were shaking and my heart was pounding; I could hardly hold the drumsticks. Then, at a nod from Bruno, I began to tap out the opening few beats to our first song and miraculously, the others joined in on time. We were up and running and much to my relief, I managed to perform both songs without any real errors. The audience seemed pleased and we received warm applause as we stood and took a bow. At the end of the evening, I was surprised to find that we had won third prize. For a brief moment, thoughts of a career as a pop star in France ran through my mind. But I quickly remembered that I was booked on a flight back to England in two days' time where home, family and school awaited me. Still, it was good to dream, if only for a few seconds.

There were sadness and tears when Claudine and I parted at St Nazaire airport at the end of August. I can't say that we truly loved each other but there was certainly deep affection between us. Although we had enjoyed being with one another and had great fun, we knew that our time together was at an end. Of course, we talked seriously about meeting up again, either at Christmas or if that wasn't possible, then very definitely, the following summer. We promised to write to each other regularly and this we did for several months. However, the letters gradually became shorter and the intervals between them longer. With the impatience of youth, we both eventually moved on to other things and other relationships and I never saw Claudine again.

Chapter Seven
LIFE IN THE UPPER SIXTH

When I returned home from France, I found my mother to be in a difficult mood and our relations were very strained for a while. I had never known my mother like this and it was hard to deal with. I didn't know if this was because she had not fully got over seeing me canoodling with Claudine or whether it was a menopausal issue (not that I understood anything about this at that time). She showed no interest in what had happened while I was away in France, which I resented and we hardly spoke to each other for a couple of weeks. It may also have simply been due to tiredness on my mother's part. I had noticed in recent months how she seemed to tire more easily than before. Eventually, things swung back onto a more even keel and life in our household returned to normal but my mother's tiredness continued. We didn't know it at the time but this was a precursor to a gradual deterioration in her health.

My mother's tiredness wasn't the only health issue we had to face at that time. In the autumn of 1963, we received some very bad news. At the age of sixteen, Fiona was diagnosed with a hole in the heart and my mother was faced with the incredibly difficult decision of whether to agree to life or death surgery. Major health complications were common among people with Down's syndrome and as a result, many of them only lived into their thirties. I think my mother had therefore always hoped that she would outlive Fiona. The doctors told my mother that there was only a 50/50 chance of Fiona surviving the operation but if she did, her life expectancy would be considerably improved and she would almost certainly outlive my mother. It was an awful dilemma for my mother but after an anguished few days, she gave the go-ahead for the operation which took place a month later. Fortunately, all went well at the hospital and the operation was totally successful. After a week in hospital to recover, Fiona returned home frail but smiling. She was left with a massive scar around her chest but the doctors assured my mother that Fiona would now be able to lead a long and healthy life. Of course, this was both good and bad news. Fiona's significantly increased life expectancy simply increased my mother's worries about the long-term future of my sister.

The situation was made even more difficult for my mother because just before Fiona's diagnosis, our friends, the Elgood family, had left Leamington to move near Maidstone in Kent. This meant that during this critical period, my mother had no-one close with whom to discuss the problem or share the burden. Along with my mother, I was also very sad to see the Elgoods leave and of course, to have to say goodbye to Robert. We had spent a lot of time together over the past few years and the Elgood family had also been an important influence in my life. Although we subsequently drove down to visit them in their new home a few times, their departure from Leamington left a big gap in the lives of both my mother and myself.

It took me quite a while to get over Claudine but one Friday in early November, I was in our favourite Italian coffee bar and found myself sitting next to a girl I'd not met before. She stood out because she was dressed in a rather 'hippy' fashion and wore a Donovan-style cap[20] which was very avant-garde for our provincial, teenaged group. I was intrigued and started up a conversation with her. She told me she had only just moved up to Leamington from the London area and was at the girl's school in Warwick. She proved to be easy to chat to and I ended up asking her to go with me to a Bonfire Night party

---

[20] Donovan was an up and coming folk-pop singer, something of a British equivalent to Bob Dylan, who always wore a peaked, fisherman-style cap.

that I had been invited to the next day. She agreed and I duly picked her up in my mother's car the next evening outside the coffee shop and we drove to the party. The evening went well, we enjoyed the fireworks and sat side-by-side around the bonfire, chatting, drinking and kissing until she said it was time for her to go. She was a little wobbly on her feet as we walked to the car but I opened the passenger door for her and helped her in. She told me where she lived and a little while later, we drew up outside her house. As I switched off the car engine and turned to put my arm around her and give her a kiss, she suddenly leaned forward and was sick all over the dashboard and into the foot-well. I gave her my handkerchief to wipe her face and then, after a brief apology, she slid out of the car and staggered into her house. It was clear that our evening together was now over and it had not ended as I had hoped. Although I saw her again in the café occasionally, all I could think about was the awful mess I had cleaned up in my mother's car. We didn't renew our brief acquaintance.

That Christmas, I managed to get a job for two weeks with the Post Office again. Most of the time, I started by sorting letters into pigeon holes for a few hours and then went out delivering one of the rounds. We were paid by the hour, so we always tried to find ways to increase our pay by finding additional work or by dragging out the time it took to do our rounds. There were quite a lot of students and casual workers employed for the Christmas rush and since the Post Office's management of our activities was rather lax, it was easy to occasionally add a bit of extra time. One afternoon, three of us were assigned to the parcel sorting office – a large hall where incoming parcels were sorted for delivery all over the country, either by rail or Post Office vans. We helped with the sorting and then carried the sacks out to the vans. After several hours of work, there was a lull in activity and we three were told by the supervisor that we wouldn't be needed any longer. He then wandered off but of course, this wasn't what we wanted to hear. We had just loaded a large van bound for Birmingham and one of us had the bright idea that we should get in the back of the van and go in it to Birmingham. Once there, we would tell the driver that we had been sent to help unload and then come back in the van. That way, we would earn several extra hours of money.

It all sounded simple and quite plausible so we rushed back outside and jumped unseen into the back of the waiting van, closing the rear doors behind us. A few minutes later, the driver got in, switched on the engine and we were off to Birmingham, as easy as that. When we arrived at the Birmingham sorting office and the driver opened up the rear doors, he was more than a little surprised to find us spread-eagled there on top of all the bags of parcels. We recited our story about having been instructed to come to help with the unloading but he was very suspicious. He called over a manager who, understandably, would have none of our story. We were quickly dispatched back to Leamington in another van and told to report to the duty manager immediately on our return. He gave us a complete dressing down and docked half our pay for that day. We couldn't complain and were lucky not to have been fired. Sometimes what appear to be good ideas don't always work out.

In my first week in the Upper Sixth, a new boy arrived in class called Andy Renton. He had just moved to Leamington from the Chester area as his father, who worked for Massey Ferguson, had taken a new job as shipping manager at their headquarters in Coventry.[21] Andy had the desk next to mine in our form room and we soon struck up a close friendship, although I'm not sure what drew us together initially. Andy and I didn't study the same subjects so we didn't spend that much time

---

[21] At the time, the Massey Ferguson facility in Banner Lane on the south side of Coventry was one of the world's largest agricultural equipment factories, producing over 70,000 tractors annually at its peak, mostly for export.

together in school and I already had two or three good school friends. He was keen on watching football, especially Liverpool which I wasn't and I liked playing tennis and hockey which he didn't. His family circumstances were also very different to mine, with a father in a well-paid job and a younger brother and sister. As I look back now, I find myself wondering what exactly is the key to making good friends and why do some friendships last while others fade over time? Although we were in the same class, the normal elements of friendship such as shared interests, similar backgrounds etc. just didn't apply to Andy and me. Despite this, we ended up being the closest of friends for many years.

At school, we sixth-formers were allowed to spend our lunchtimes in the sixth form common room doing more or less whatever we chose – reading, chatting, listening to music and playing cards. A few of the boys started playing bridge regularly which was a game I'd not seen before. It intrigued me and as I enjoyed cards, I decided to join in, quickly followed by Andy. Neither of us knew how to play at first but we soon picked up the basics from the other boys. I found a small book on teach yourself bridge in a second-hand book shop which helped improve our game. Once we got into it, we were hooked and a few weeks later, we formed our own little bridge club with two other friends, Colin Sheldon and Mark Ryan. We were soon meeting quite regularly at weekends at one of our houses. The ability to play bridge turned out to be a good skill that proved useful in later life. Some may think it a little strange that four, active young men would spend Saturday nights playing bridge, even if it was accompanied by a few beers. The simple truth was that we had fun – our bridge was never that serious and we enjoyed a sort of camaraderie that only comes when you're with people you like and respect. Also, we only arranged our bridge nights when there were no other interesting social activities going on such as parties or dances.

Although Andy and I didn't spend that much time together in school, at weekends I would regularly go around to his house to spend time with him and his family. I went to watch my first football match with him at Coventry City's ground. His dad had tickets and drove us there in style in his fancy, black company car – a Humber I think. We invariably spent Saturday night in each other's company. We usually met in one of Leamington's pubs where we would join up with a group of friends and check whether there was anything special happening that night. On the slightest hint or rumour that something might be going on in the area, we would zoom off in our cars to investigate. Occasionally, we got lucky but more often than not, we simply ended up racing around the Warwickshire countryside on a pub crawl. By today's standards, our attitudes towards drinking and driving would be considered rash and stupid but the issue of drink-driving was not the regarded in the same serious manner that it was some years later. In our defence, I should say that there was much less traffic on the roads then and as far as I am aware, none of us was ever involved in a crash during these weekend escapades.

In the broader world beyond our suburban lives in Leamington, major events such as the Cuban missile crisis, the assassination of President Kennedy and rising tensions between the Israelis and Arabs or the situation in Vietnam filled our newspapers at the time. Although they had no direct impact on what we did as schoolboys, they did give us cause for concern and were always discussed as topical events in our General Studies lessons. We were old enough with sufficient maturity to be able to debate the issues and I well recall the worried discussions about the likelihood of a nuclear Armageddon while Kennedy and Khrushchev faced off each other. The few boys amongst us who still had bomb shelters in their gardens from World War II suddenly became very popular.

A few weeks before I was due to sit my 'A' levels, I gave up my job at the chemist shop in order to concentrate on my studies. I was reasonably confident about the upcoming exams since I was expected to get an A grade in geography, a B in French, English Literature and General Studies, I thought this would be enough to see me gain a place at one of my four chosen universities and over the course of a couple of weeks in June, I duly sat my exams. Although I found some parts hard, on balance they were no more difficult than was to be expected. However, when the results came out a month later, I was shocked to find that I had only achieved grade E in English, French and geography plus a B grade in General Studies. I was not the only one to be shocked as several other boys also obtained much lower grades than expected. In addition, I was the only boy in the whole class to pass geography. With such poor results, there was an enquiry at school led by the headmaster and both the senior geography and French masters were demoted. That didn't help me as I now found myself understandably rejected by each of my chosen universities.

Several of my friends had also failed to find a university place that summer, including Andy Renton, Frank Riley and Mark Ryan. Having discussed matters with the headmaster and my mother, it was agreed that I would return to school for a third year in the Sixth Form to re-sit geography and French in the summer of next year. The hope was that I could improve my results and so re-apply for a university place. I knew it would be difficult as at that time, only around five percent of school children went on to university but I was determined to try again. Andy, Frank and Mark also decided to return for an extra year together with another four or five boys. The only small consolation for all my work was that I was awarded the annual geography prize at school but since I was the only one to pass 'A' level, there wasn't anyone else they could give it to.

As I was doing some research for this book, I came across a file that contained all my old school reports from Leamington College. Reading through them again after all these years, I have to admit that I am quite surprised at the number of duties and activities in which I was apparently involved. As well as playing hockey in the school first XI, I also played chess for the school plus cricket, rugby and hockey for my House and took up golf in the sixth form. I acted in several school plays including taking the lead role of Henry VIII in *A Man for all Seasons.*[22] At various times, it seems I was a form absentee monitor, ran the lost property office, a librarian in the main school library as well as the senior librarian for the sixth form library, a lateness monitor and eventually a prefect. I just don't remember my school days being so busy or useful.

---

[22] I followed up my success in *A Man for all Seasons* by joining the local theatre in Leamington, The Loft and had minor roles in several plays.

Chapter Eight
Teaching and Travel

Having failed in my attempt to enter university, I returned to school in September 1963 for the autumn term to brush up my geography and to acquaint myself with the new course books for French. On the advice of my geography master, I decided to try to supplement these two, repeat 'A' levels by also taking economics. The subject wasn't taught at our school but I found out that it was possible to attend weekly night school classes for economics at the Warwickshire College of Further Education in Leamington. The course was designed for local council employees to give them a general understanding of the subject but I was told by the teacher that with a little extra work on my part, it should give me a sufficient base to take the 'A' level exam. I had to pay to attend and also cover the cost of taking the exam but it seemed to me it would be worth the expense. So, I enrolled on the course and spent three hours almost every Wednesday evening until the following June at the College.

I remained good friends with Andy Renton and we still went out together most weekends. When we could afford it, we started occasionally going to a hotel a few miles outside Leamington that had recently introduced a live band with dancing on Saturday nights. I did the driving and Andy paid half the petrol cost. Apart from the music, the main motivation for going was to try to pick up girls but sadly, with a couple of exceptions, we were not terribly successful. I once joked with Andy that things would be much better if one of us was a girl. I don't think it was a lack of charm or wit that held us back. It was more to do with the fact that we were at the younger end of the spectrum of those attending, so most girls were older than us. Also, the girls expected the men to pay for their drinks and with our limited resources, it was hard for us to compete with the older boys.

For a while, I partially solved this problem by arranging a BYO (bring your own). I began going out with a girl called Carol who I had originally met while still working at the chemist shop earlier that year. She was doing a Saturday job like me, but was a counter sales assistant. Carol was a year younger than me, with shoulder-length blonde hair, a petite figure and evidently, very interested in boys. Although we spent more time than we should have chatting away to each other each Saturday, she seemed to have no shortage of boyfriends and I never quite had the courage to ask her out. By pure chance, I met her again that autumn at a party. We started talking and ended up spending the evening together. I invited her out again the following weekend and along with Andy, I took her dancing to the hotel outside Leamington. We got on fine initially and repeated our dancing date several times over the ensuing couple of months but then things started to go awry. Despite the fact that she appeared very sexy and had apparently had plenty of experience with boys, she either didn't want to, or know how to, kiss properly. When we kissed, her teeth remained firmly clenched and she kept her hands stiffly at her sides so that any kissing with her wasn't a very pleasant experience. In this sense, she was something of a tease, promising more than she delivered. Eventually, with no development in our relationship, we grew bored with each other and stopped going out together.

Late that summer, I received a letter from my paternal grandmother in Toronto telling me that she would shortly be visiting Europe and suggesting we could meet while she was staying in London. I hadn't seen my grandmother since we left Toronto many years before and although she had subsequently sent me the occasional Christmas card, I had no clear recollections of her. However, I thought I thought I should make the effort to meet her and renew our family ties and so, one September morning, I drove down to London to see her. She was staying in a posh hotel close to Hyde Park Corner and we had agreed to meet for tea in the restaurant. It was a strange but pleasant experience. Not having seen each other for almost fifteen years, the conversation was difficult at first but my grandmother proved to be an easy person to chat to and we got on well together. She updated me on news about my father and Aunt Bonnie-Jean and I did the same regarding my mother and Fiona. We parted after a couple of hours, promising to try to stay in touch a little more regularly. As I drove home that evening, I had very mixed emotions. I was happy to have had the chance to meet my grandmother but felt sad that I might not see her again and regretted once again our overall family situation.

As the autumn term drew to a close and the Christmas of 1963 approached, I felt I had done enough schooling. I continued with my night school course and still did some studying at home to prepare for my 'A' level exams the following summer but I thought I should now get a job. I was conscious that it had been a difficult decision for my mother to allow me to stay on in the sixth form instead of starting work and I felt I should try to earn my keep. At that time, it was occasionally possible for boys waiting to enter university to take up a position as a student teacher. This was a programme run by some County Councils to allow students to gain some experience of teaching in order to encourage them to take this up as a career after graduating. I duly applied to Warwickshire County Council to find out if there were any vacancies and after attending an interview, I was very pleased and somewhat surprised to be offered a job at my former junior school in Milverton. It was a full-time role starting in January and running through until the end of the school year in July. The best news was that I would be paid a salary of just over £60 each month. For the very first time, I would have real money in my pocket and be able to make a proper contribution to the household finances.

It felt very weird going back to my old school on the first day of term. The place was full of memories, the assembly hall, the same classroom where I had once sat and the playground where I used to run around with the other children. Fortunately, perhaps, none of the current teachers had been at the school when I was there. Now I was the teacher at the front of the class with dozens of eyes gazing expectantly at me. My initial duties mainly involved standing in for any teachers who were off sick or away on courses, doing special reading classes for some of the more backward children plus supervising most of the school sporting activities. However, after a couple of months, one of the male teachers became seriously ill with a virus and the headmaster asked if I would be willing to take over his class until he returned. Although it would be a challenge, the headmaster clearly felt I was up to the task and so, full of the confidence of youth, I said yes.

My class, as they now became, consisted of some thirty-odd lively ten and eleven years old pupils and they were, on the whole, a joy to teach. I soon mastered their curriculum and discipline was rarely an issue. Indeed, I was secretly pleased to note that adjacent classes sometimes seemed noisier and more out of control than mine. Although I now had my own full-time class, I continued to take most of the sporting activities. Other than the playground, which was used for girl's netball, the school didn't have any sports facilities so a couple of afternoons each week, I found myself back in Victoria Park. I used to walk down from Milverton to the park carrying a canvas bag of sports equipment, accompanied by some thirty to forty boisterous children. Once there, I organised them into groups for games. Rounders proved to be the most popular, as it was suitable for both boys and girls of all ages and luckily for me, it didn't require much equipment. I often joined in, much to the delight of the kids. After a couple of hours of fun, we all trudged back up the hill to Milverton, returning for the end of the school day.

During the summer term, I became friends with one of the female teachers called Martha, who was only two or three years older than me. She had only just completed her teacher's training course and had moved to Leamington to start in this, her first job. As we close in age, we often sat together chatting during the morning break or at lunch and Martha was very helpful in giving me advice about how to handle the children and the curriculum. Then one afternoon, out of the blue, she invited me to join her for tea the following Saturday in her flat. I was caught by surprise and not sure initially what to say. I was still quite inexperienced in relationships between adult males and females and unsure whether this was simply a friendly invitation to tea or whether something more serious was afoot. I knew from the odd remark she had made during our lunch-time chats that she hadn't made any close friends yet in Leamington but I hesitated to think that she might be attracted to me. Martha was older than me and a real woman, with a shapely figure, not a giggly young teenager like my few previous female acquaintances. I decided, however, to take things as they appeared on the surface and accepted a friendly invitation to tea.

Martha gave me her address and it turned out her flat was immediately opposite the Victoria Park, so easy for me to find. I arranged with my mother to borrow her car for the Saturday afternoon and so drove down from Lillington for my teachers' tea-time rendezvous. The event passed off ordinarily enough initially. Martha had laid on a pleasant tea and we enjoyed each other's company for a couple of hours, sitting side by side, chatting about the other teachers and exchanging information about life in Leamington. But, although inexperienced, I wasn't stupid and as the afternoon wore on, I could tell from the way Martha looked at me and the closeness of her body next to mine on the couch that she was hoping or intending that things might move beyond small-talk. I became increasingly nervous and was unsure what to do. Then, as we talked, our arms touched and before I knew it, we were holding hands and looking into each other's eyes. Her face was just a few inches from mine and below it, I could see her breasts gently heaving under her white blouse. After a few moments, we kissed several times, lightly, not passionately. As a young man, I was attracted to Martha – she was quite good-looking and easy to talk to. But I felt uneasy about having a relationship with a fellow teacher and an older woman. I wasn't ready for this. I don't know whether Martha sensed some reluctance on my part or if she also had second thoughts as she then said quietly, 'I think it's time you went.' She was right and I was soon in my car driving back home, ruminating on what might have been. We remained friends in school but never repeated our tea-time intimacy.

Towards the end of June, the headmaster asked me one day if I was willing to come back after the summer break until I (hopefully) went up to university in October. Although the teacher who had been away ill was due to return in September, the headmaster explained that they would appreciate my continued help with the remedial reading classes and running the sports activities. He also went on to say that if I returned, I would of course be paid through the six weeks of the summer holidays. This was an unexpected but very welcome bonus; my mind was instantly made up and I duly agreed to return to Milverton for one final month of teaching.

With the certainty of my teaching income during the summer holidays, I made up my mind to give my mother a break and take her on a holiday somewhere before I went off to university. We discussed the idea one evening and she seemed quite enthusiastic about the idea, telling me that she would like to drive over to the Continent, to visit France or maybe Spain. The only problem was Fiona. I didn't want to deny her a holiday but felt strongly that my mother needed a rest and some time off from looking after my sister. We eventually agreed that my mother would approach the council's social services and see if they could find somewhere for Fiona to stay for a week or so. They responded positively and within a week, we had confirmation that Fiona could stay at a care home just outside Leamington. With that issue resolved, I realised that I would need to find an additional job if I was to fund a holiday across the Channel. After searching through the local newspaper the next day, I saw that a local taxi company was looking for additional drivers for the busy holiday period. I immediately telephoned them, arranged an interview and after some hesitation about my young age and lack of experience, the manager offered me a job. I should point out that at that time, taxi drivers were not required to have a PSV licence.

I turned up again the following morning and was duly assigned a black cab to drive. After a few instructions about how things worked, I was sent off to work the main taxi rank by the town hall in central Leamington. It proved to be a relatively straight-forward job, though boring at times – I got through several books over the next six weeks or so. Most of the time, I either simply waited at the rank for a fare or responded to a call from the dispatcher to pick someone up from an address elsewhere in town. I knew Leamington and the surrounding area fairly well from all my years delivering my mother's dressmaking output so it was usually easy to find my way around. The only real problems were the lunch-time drunks who wanted a taxi home in the early afternoon. Sometimes they couldn't remember where they lived, sometimes I had to help them out of the taxi and in through their front door and sometimes they didn't have enough money left for the fare. Just occasionally though, they made up for all this by giving me an excellent tip.

I did get the occasional longer journey which were always sought after by the drivers because of the higher fares and bigger tips. My most challenging occurred one day when I was working the rank outside the main station in Leamington. An agitated man with his wife and two children came running up to my black cab and asked if I could take them to Banbury station. They had just missed their train to London and there wasn't another one due for four hours but if I could get them to Banbury within an hour, they could make a connection there. I had never been to Banbury and had no idea where the station was or how long it would take to get there but I wasn't about to pass up such an opportunity. I quickly consulted with a couple of the other drivers who told me it was just about possible to drive there in an hour. They gave me brief directions on how to reach Banbury and find the station. So, I went back to the family and told them to jump in, assuring them confidently that we would get there in time. We set off to a screech of tyres and headed out of town. I drove as fast as I could, with my heart pounding, desperately trying to remember the set of directions I had been given. Happily, the traffic on the roads was fairly light and after a couple of missed turns in the centre of Banbury, I found the station and deposited my passengers outside with some five minutes to spare. The man was duly appreciative and tipped me well.

While I was doing my taxi driving job, my 'A' level results came out. I was delighted to find that I had obtained B grades in all three subjects that I had sat – Economics, geography and French. When combined with my English and General Studies results from the previous summer, I was now certain that with five 'A' levels I should be able to go on to university. Since I didn't have an offer from anywhere, I was advised to apply for a place through the university clearing house system, which I duly did, just a few days before my mother and I left on holiday. This meant I would have to wait until I returned to find out the result of my application.

We set off bright and early one mid-August morning in my mother's white Morris Minor convertible and headed down the M45 and M1 towards London and the south coast. We had no firm plans, other than to catch a late afternoon ferry from Dover and then head south wherever the open road would take us. We caught our ferry without any problems, arriving in Calais in the early evening. Once through passport control, I headed our car away from the docks in the direction of Paris and drove on until it was fully dark. We spent the night in a lay-by somewhere along the road and then after a good French breakfast in a nearby café, I continued driving south. I asked my mother what she wanted to do – stop off in France or go on to Spain. We were both excited about visiting General Franco's Spain[23] so we just kept on going. By the time that we crossed the Spanish border early that evening, I was extremely tired, having done some twelve hours of almost non-stop driving on very busy French Route Nationales. So, as we made our way along the coast with night falling, we headed into San Sebastian and decided to stop there overnight. We quickly found a pleasant, modern hotel on the sea front and after a simple dinner, we were both soon in bed and fast asleep.

Luckily, our choice of hotel proved to be a good one. We had a room overlooking the sea, there was a large swimming pool, the food and service in the restaurant were fine and as we had hoped, the weather was hot and sunny. I did some quick calculations that morning and reckoned that I had enough cash to pay for four nights in the hotel so we decided to stay where we were. At that time, Spain was only slowly emerging from its Fascist, totalitarian past with General Franco still very much ruling the roost. Life in Spain remained very controlled; there were police everywhere, bikinis were banned as were all the regional languages such as Basque and Catalan. Coastal resorts like San Sebastian were relatively quiet places, mostly used only by the Spanish. As far as we were aware, there was only one other British family at the hotel during our stay - the ubiquitous package tour industry had not really got going here yet.

Our time in Spain ended far too quickly and I wasn't particularly looking forward to the long haul back to Calais. In the end, however, the return journey proved uneventful and we arrived home in Lillington in the late afternoon the following day. Looking back now, I am amazed at how casually we treated the whole trip. Apart

---

[23] General Franco was a military dictator who ruled Spain from 1939 until his death in 1975.

from buying European insurance cover for the car, a GB sticker and French road map, I don't think we did anything else to prepare. We had no problems getting on the cross-channel ferries, we changed money as we went along, we didn't get seriously lost and it was easy finding a hotel in San Sebastian, even in August. Fortunately, our little Morris Minor covered the 1700 miles of our journey without missing a beat. I was glad that I had made the effort to take my mother away – it was her first holiday in almost fifteen years and she had obviously enjoyed her adventure.

As soon as we arrived back home, I had to urgently tackle the issue of my future. Waiting for me on the doorstep was a letter advising me I had been offered a provisional place at Sheffield University, subject to attending an interview there in just two days' time. I had never been further north in Britain than Birmingham and so quickly retrieved my UK road map from the car to see exactly where Sheffield was. I reckoned I could there and back by car in a day, so I telephoned the university to confirm my intention to attend the interview. Two days later, I set off in my mother's Morris Minor accompanied by my friend, Mark Ryan, to help with the cross-country navigation. All went well. After a very short interview, I was immediately offered a place on the geography honours course, which was exactly what I wanted. Mark and I were back in Leamington without any problems by early evening. I had finally achieved my objective and felt very proud. It would be my twentieth birthday in a couple of days and now I had something to really celebrate, even if it had taken me a year longer than expected. The summer of '56 had been a watershed moment in my life and now, eight years later, the summer of '64 was proving to be an equally important time of change. In a month's time, I would be at university and yet another stage in my life was about to begin.

Postscripts

And Subsequently ….

A few years after my parents divorced, my father married a younger woman he had met in Toronto called Nan. On his retirement at the ripe old age of fifty, they moved to Vancouver where they subsequently had a daughter, my half-sister Sally. My father and I have remained in touch all these years both through visits and letters and at the time of writing, my father is still alive and we are planning to attend his 100th birthday party. My mother did not re-marry and continued to live quietly with Fiona in Lillington. In the mid-1960s, my mother's health began to noticeably deteriorate. Heavy colds and occasional 'flu seemed to affect her more than in the past. I think she was simply worn out from a life-time of hard work. She eventually contracted breast cancer and after two very difficult years, died in hospital in 1973, a few months after her sixtieth birthday.

Having survived her major heart operation, Fiona, as predicted, outlived my mother by a considerable margin. After my mother's death, Fiona lived for while in a care home near Leamington and then moved into sheltered accommodation run by the council which was just around the corner from Milverton school where I once taught. I visited her regularly over the years and once I returned to the UK from working overseas, she used to come to stay with me periodically. She was well looked after in Leamington until her death in late 2016 at the age of sixty-nine.

After Brian married and moved to Birmingham, he never came back to see us in Leamington. He remained in touch with Pat sporadically and she passed on any news to us. In the early seventies, I occasionally drove through Birmingham while working and called in on Brian a couple of times in 1972 or 1973. He was renting a very dingy flat in the Smethwick area and had clearly gone downhill since his wife left. He was unemployed, just doing odd jobs to get by and I felt very sorry for him. I tried to help him but soon after my last visit, I moved overseas and never saw or heard from him again. Pat remained in Kenilworth and her married life was fine for a while but then she had a brief affair with a neighbour, ended up getting pregnant and had a baby. This eventually caused a break-up of her marriage. I last saw Pat at my mother's funeral in 1973 but didn't hear from her again until a brief telephone call in 1995. She was still in Kenilworth.

After our meeting in London in 1963, I did in fact see my paternal grandmother again – this time while I was on a visit to Toronto. Whilst there, I also saw my Aunt Bonnie-Jean who had recently married. My grandmother eventually died in a Toronto nursing home in her early-nineties.

Mrs Hussey visited us occasionally in Lillington but neither her son Dennis, nor Mr Hussey, ever came with her. The last time I saw her in 1963, Mrs Hussey looked older but a little more relaxed and happier as her husband was drinking less. Dennis had left school a few years earlier to join the local Gas Board as an apprentice fitter.

After three or four years in Maidstone, the Elgood family moved to Lincoln and in 1965, I drove my mother, Fiona and my girlfriend and future wife to visit them there. I happened to be in Lincoln again in the early 1990s and called in at their house and was lucky to find Mrs Elgood at home. She told me Dr Elgood had retired, Mary was happily married and living in Northampton and that Robert had also married and was living in Florence, Italy. While researching this book, I discovered that Robert, like me, has also written several books and he is now a world authority on the arms and armour of the Islamic world.

Andy Renton and I remained good friends for some years. We even shared a flat in Manchester for a year while I was working there and he was doing an MBA at

Salford University. He went on to work for Ford in Dagenham in the HR department and we attended each other's weddings but once I moved overseas, we sadly lost touch with each other.

In her last letter to me, Claudine, my one-time French girlfriend wrote to tell me she was now going out with Bruno, he of the battered, old Fiat 500. I have no idea whether their relationship lasted but I did go back to La Baule as promised, two summers after we parted. I was on holiday, driving around Brittany for a few days with Robert Elgood and we stopped at the beach-side cottage that Claudine's family had rented. I had hoped that the family might have been there again that year but different people were in residence and sadly, they knew nothing of Claudine or her family.

As for me, the years described in this book were my most formative ones and helped determine the person that I am today. As far as the evergreen argument about nature or nurture is concerned, I have no doubt that I have inherited traits from both my parents as well as being greatly influenced by my upbringing. I was generally happy at Kenilworth Road but our relocation to Lillington in the summer of 1956 was a shock that took some years to get over. I never really felt at home there and, although sad to leave my mother and Fiona, I was glad when I was able to leave for university in 1964. After graduating in economics, I began a career in industry, married a girl from Yorkshire, had three sons and travelled the world. The rest as they say, is history.

Reflections on Life Then and Now

Looking back now on my early childhood years more than half a century later, I am reminded just how different our lives were in the late 1940s and 1950s compared to those of my own children and the generations that have followed in our footsteps. In many respects, our lives then were closer to and more comparable with those of people who lived in the 1920s and 1930s. Although jobs were more plentiful after the War, the fundamentals of society had remained largely unchanged - the overall standard of living, general social habits, the type and quality of housing plus the importance of religious belief and regular church attendance. On Sundays, shops were closed as well as most forms of entertainment, there were hardly any supermarkets and virtually everyone listened regularly to the radio as eagerly as they did before the War.

My later childhood saw the start of the many important changes that were to transform British society from the 1960s onwards – increasing home and car ownership, easier overseas travel, rising wages and living standards, the wider affordability of domestic appliances, a broader diet, the rise in university admissions plus the arrival of mass television and the emerging pop culture. Improving health and especially longer life expectancy also played an important role in how society developed. These significant changes simultaneously reflected the population's growing desire for a better life as well as facilitating society's ability to achieve it. All this culminated in the so-called 'swinging sixties' – a time when so many fundamental changes in society seemed to come together.

For me, the fundamental differences between our lives during the period of this book compared with those of the modern day can be generally summarized into four key areas.

More certainty – less choice.
More cohesion – less individualism.
More religion – less tolerance.
More hope – less expectation.

In the 1950s and early 1960s, people generally knew their position in society and how life would most likely turn out. Almost everyone who wanted to work could find a job and afford somewhere to live in a reasonably safe environment. From that base, they could expect to marry, aspire to live in their own home and have children who could benefit from free education and a decent health system. There was however, much less choice and considerably less social mobility. Where to live and what employment to choose, whether to stay married or divorce, access to the legal system, the number of holidays and where to spend them, the range and type of food available in the shops or restaurants and the alternatives as to how to spend one's limited leisure time were all much more limited then.

In many ways, life was much more institutionalised then in the sense that the major public institutions were more respected and had more impact on and control over people's lives. This resulted in a more stable, cohesive society with generally shared values and well-understood rules that were largely common across society. Communities and families were also generally much closer then. However, there was not the freedom of expression and the ability to be different that are to be found in today's society. The political scene was much more homogeneous, dominated by the either the Conservatives or Labour and quite different from the diversity of parties and views that are seen today. The police and other figures in authority were more respected and therefore more influential. Also, conscription was still in force so most young men had some experience of serving in the armed forces. By being taken out of their immediate home environment and thrown together with a group of strangers, it was a great equalizer that helped many young men to better handle life in general. It also provided those who perhaps had not done so well at school a chance to learn some basic skills for later finding a job in 'civvy' street.

Religion was vastly more important in most people's lives in the 1950's and whether Catholic, Jew or Protestant, most adults attended church at least once a week. However, this fact masked some very narrow-minded attitudes about how people should behave or live their lives, whether in public or private. Society in general was much less tolerant of differences or deviation from the 'accepted norm', whether these related to divorce, unmarried mothers, homosexuality or disability. People were expected to conform and those who didn't were largely looked down on or marginalized by the rest of society.

Whether by nature or force of circumstance, people were more self-reliant, generally believing or hoping that life's challenges could be handled by themselves or their immediate family circle. There was less expectation that the State or society would provide or regulate in their favour. The panoply of government support available today, pensions, sickness pay, maternity and unemployment benefits etc. were much more restricted then. Even though many people held aspirations, most simply had lower expectations of what life and society in general would deliver. Although people were often unhappy or worried and might complain about their situation or problems, this was largely contained or limited to family and friends. It was a vastly different situation from the level of litigation and the frequency of formal complaints we see these days.

In making these comparisons, I offer no judgement about which period and life-style was best. All I know is that much of my childhood was generally happy, in spite of the challenges we faced as a family and for that, I am deeply indebted to my mother. At the end of the day, we have to do our best with the hand we are dealt in life. With a little luck, hope and ambition most of us have the opportunity to use whatever talents we possess to achieve some fulfilment and happiness in our lives and those around us.

Chester August 2017